ASPECTS OF THE
MASCULINE

from

The Collected Works of C. G. Jung

Volumes 4, 5, 7, 8, 9 i, 10, 13, 14

BOLLINGEN SERIES XX

C. G. Jung: Letters

BOLLINGEN SERIES XCV

C. G. Jung Speaking

BOLLINGEN SERIES XCVII

C. G. Jung: Seminar on Dream Analysis

BOLLINGEN SERIES XCIX

ASPECTS
OF THE
MASCULINE

C. G. JUNG

TRANSLATED BY R.F.C. HULL
INTRODUCTION
AND HEADNOTES
BY JOHN BEEBE

BOLLINGEN SERIES

PRINCETON UNIVERSITY PRESS

Extracts from the Collected Works of C. G. Jung: "The Origin of the Hero" and "The Battle for Deliverance from the Mother," Volume 5, *Symbols of Transformation*, copyright © 1956 by Bollingen Foundation, Inc. "The Stages of Life," Volume 8, *The Structure and Dynamics of the Psyche*, copyright © 1960 by Bollingen Foundation, Second Edition copyright © 1969 by Princeton University Press. "On the Psychology of the Unconscious" and "The Personal and the Collective Unconscious," Volume 7, *Two Essays on Analytical Psychology*, copyright © 1953 by Bollingen Foundation, Inc., new material copyright © 1966 by Bollingen Foundation. "The Love Problem of a Student," Volume 10, *Civilization in Transition*, copyright © 1964 by Bollingen Foundation, Second Edition copyright © 1970 by Princeton University Press. "The Significance of the Father in the Destiny of the Individual," Volume 4, *Freud and Psychoanalysis*, copyright © 1961 by Bollingen Foundation. "The Personification of the Opposites," Volume 14, *Mysterium Coniunctionis*, copyright © 1963 by Bollingen Foundation, Second Edition copyright © 1970 by Princeton University Press. "Concerning the Archetypes with Special Reference to the Anima Concept" and "The Phenomenology of the Spirit in Fairytales," Volume 9, i, *The Archetypes and the Collective Unconscious*, copyright © 1959 by Bollingen Foundation, Inc., new material copyright © 1969 by Bollingen Foundation. "The Spirit Mercurius," Volume 13, *Alchemical Studies*, copyright © 1967 by Bollingen Foundation.

Extracts from other sources: "Lecture VIII, 13 March 1929, Dream [12]" and "Lecture V, 19 February 1930, Dream [23]," *Seminar on Dream Analysis*, copyright © 1984 by Princeton University Press. "Letter of 12 November 1957," Volume 2 of the *C. G. Jung: Letters*, copyright © 1975 by Princeton University Press. "Letter of 26 August 1943," Volume 1 of the *C. G. Jung: Letters*, copyright © 1973 by Princeton University Press. "The Houston Films" (© 1964 and 1976 by Richard I. Evans) and "Esther Harding's Notebooks" (© 1975 by C. G. Jung Foundation for Analytical Psychology, Inc.), *C. G. Jung Speaking*, copyright © 1977 by Princeton University Press.

All the volumes composing the Collected Works constitute number XX in Bollingen Series, under the editorship of Herbert Read, Michael Fordham, and Gerhard Adler; executive editor, William McGuire. *Seminar on Dream Analysis*, Bollingen Series XCIX, edited by William McGuire. *C. G. Jung: Letters*, Volumes 1 and 2, Bollingen Series XCV, under the editorship of Gerhard Adler and Aniela Jaffé, and translated by R.F.C. Hull. *C. G. Jung Speaking*, Bollingen Series XCVII, edited by William McGuire and R.F.C. Hull.

LIBRARY OF CONGRESS CATALOG NUMBER: 88-37903

ISBN 0-691-01884-7

PRINTED IN THE UNITED STATES OF AMERICA

First Princeton/Bollingen Paperback Edition, 1989

TABLE OF CONTENTS

EDITOR'S INTRODUCTION

To understand what C. G. Jung means by "the masculine" is to gain access to the ground of his entire approach to psychology, for his psychology, as he liked to admit, was his "personal confession"—the confession of a man seeking to understand human psychology in the patriarchal context of a private practice in a western European country in the first half of the twentieth century. Not even the demonstrable universality of the archetypal world that he uncovered in this endeavor could eliminate the human standpoint of the pioneer, who remained a man telling us what *his* experience had been. Therefore the present collection of excerpts from his writings affords an opportunity to discover what Jung himself understood of the contribution that gender made to his "personal equation," a chance to look at the lens of the telescope through which he made his famous and far-reaching observations of the major psychological constellations.

Surprisingly, with the exception of the very early essay, "On the Significance of the Father in the Destiny of the Individual," written when he was still a Freudian psychoanalyst, there is no single published work in which Jung devotes himself exclusively to either the psychology of men or the broader unconscious psychology of the masculine. There is neither a monograph detailing a man's process of psychological development nor an essay devoted to the animus, the masculine archetype that Jung interpreted for women as their soul-image. One has to pick one's way through many essays to uncover the thread of meaning that conveys Jung's own masculine path through the labyrinth of the unconscious. The present selection, though far from the only one possible, is an attempt to reveal this thread to the reader who wants to follow Jung's track.

The path unfolds from Jung's own childhood experiences in a vicarage as the son of a pastor who was losing his faith and the confidence of his wife and son. Paul Jung was both blocked and incapable of the kind of self-reflection that could have unlocked his spirit; for the child Jung, with his enormous potential for psychological development, this father was an unsatisfactory figure with whom to identify. In his extraordinary imaginal autobiography, *Memories, Dreams, Reflections,* Jung gives us a glimpse of the degree to which he had to found his own identity upon a private vision of the numinous power of the masculine. This vision of archetypal masculinity was of the kind that comes to a child who has at hand no human role model to incarnate the archetypal image and mediate its power and meaning:

> . . . I had the earliest dream I can remember, a dream which was to preoccupy me all my life . . . (when) I was . . . between three and four years old.
> The vicarage stood quite alone near Laufen castle, and there was a big meadow stretching back from the sexton's farm. In the dream I was in this meadow. Suddenly I discovered a dark, rectangular, stone-lined hole in the ground. I had never seen it before. I ran forward curiously and peered down into it. Then I saw a stone stairway leading down. Hesitantly and fearfully, I descended. At the bottom was a doorway with a round arch, closed off by a green curtain. It was a big, heavy curtain of worked stuff like brocade, and it looked very sumptuous. Curious to see what might be hidden behind, I pushed it aside. I saw before me in the dim light a rectangular chamber about thirty feet long. The ceiling was arched and of hewn stone. The floor was laid with flagstones, and in the center a red carpet ran from the entrance to a low platform. On this platform stood a wonderfully rich golden throne. I am not certain, but perhaps a red cushion lay on the seat. It was a magnificent throne, a real king's throne in a fairy tale. Something was standing on it which I thought at first was a tree trunk twelve to fifteen feet high and about one and a half to two feet thick. It was a huge thing, reaching almost to the ceiling. But it was of a curious composition: it was made of skin and naked flesh, and on top there was something like a rounded head with no face and no hair. On the very top of the head was a single eye, gazing motionlessly upward.
> It was fairly light in the room, although there were no windows and no apparent source of light. Above the head, however, was an aura of brightness. The thing did not move, yet I

had the feeling that it might at any moment crawl off the throne like a worm and creep toward me. I was paralyzed with terror. At that moment I heard from outside and above my mother's voice. She called out, "Yes, just look at him. That is the man-eater!" That intensified my terror still more, and I awoke sweating and scared to death. For many nights afterward I was afraid to go to sleep, because I feared I might have another dream like that.

This dream haunted me for years. Only much later did I realize that what I had seen was a phallus, and it was decades before I understood that it was a ritual phallus. . . .

The abstract significance of the phallus is shown by the fact that it was enthroned by itself, "ithyphallically" ('ιφυς, "upright"). The hole in the meadow probably represented a grave. The grave itself was an underground temple whose green curtain symbolized the meadow, in other words the mystery of earth with her covering of green vegetation. The carpet was *blood-red*. What about the vault? Perhaps I had already been to the Munot, the citadel of Schaffhausen? This is not likely, since no one would take a three-year-old child up there. So it cannot be a memory trace. Equally, I do not know where the anatomically correct phallus can have come from. The interpretation of the *orificium urethrae* as an eye, with the source of light apparently above it, points to the etymology of the word phallus (φαλος, shining, bright).

At all events, the phallus of this dream seems to be a subterranean God "not to be named," and such it remained throughout my youth, reappearing when anyone spoke too loudly about Lord Jesus. Lord Jesus never became quite real for me, never quite acceptable, never quite lovable, for again and again I would think of his underground counterpart, a frightful revelation which had been accorded me without my seeking it.[1]

How the atmosphere of the nineteenth-century Swiss parsonage emerges from Jung's recounting of this dream and his much later associations to it! We are returned to a now-vanished late Refor-

[1] C. G. Jung, *Memories, Dreams, Reflections*, recorded and ed. Aniela Jaffé, trans. Richard and Clara Winston (New York: Pantheon, 1963), pp. 11-13.

mation world in which the bodies of the parents were never seen, and the anatomical fact of the erect penis with its urethral orifice was a religious secret, a delicate matter to be broached only in the church languages of Greek and Latin, with their mythological overtones. Growing up in this repressive atmosphere, Jung was destined to meet his masculinity archetypally, and the energy with which the archetype presented itself led him to a healing understanding of what it means to be a man that is unparalleled in the psychological literature. But because Jung's approach to the masculine was so archetypal (so underground, in the language of this dream), it is easy for its relevance to the psychology of everyday men and women to remain buried. Therefore some introduction is needed to the contents of this volume to make Jung's important insights more accessible.

The most important of these insights is the association of masculinity with the process of becoming conscious, in the Socratic sense of seeing one's existence for what it is. The equation of masculinity with consciousness is implied in the etymological linkage of phallus to brightness, and the creative child's association of the phallic opening with an eye. This early intuition was one-sided in that it left out the feminine contribution to consciousness; but its peculiarly monocular insight into the phallic nature of the psyche was essential for the development of Jung's thought. It became the basis of Jung's first attempt to find a different metaphor for the psyche's drama than the Oedipus mythologem that Freud offered. Oedipus implied the doctrine of repression, an eventual self-blinding of the human in the face of the intolerable imposed upon him by the gods. From Oedipus's story had come notions of the dream as a necessarily disguised revelation and of the psyche as something to be unmasked by a technically skilled analyst against formidable resistances. This mythologem left out the pressure from within to become conscious, which for Jung was the strongest drive of the psyche, stronger than sex or the will to power. Jung's image of the developing ego in *Wandlungen und Symbole der Libido* was not of a guilt-ridden executive bent on repressing his knowledge of shameful libidinal experience, but rather of a determined solar hero whose quest through the night sea was to maintain and increase his light against the deep instinctual forces threatening to extinguish his consciousness. (Ironically, Jung found this masculine image in the unconscious material of a woman on the brink of a psychosis.) That his hero was, like Oedipus, inflated, with a dangerous masculine arrogance in the face of the dark and lunar feminine, was anything but apparent to the thirty-six-year-old Jung who had dared to challenge Freud with his own more optimistic view of the evolutionary possibilities of ego-consciousness.

Freud's rejection of these ideas (and of the self-important way in which Jung chose to present them to the psychoanalytic world) and the concurrent uncertainty of a marital crisis brought Jung out of his youthful identification with the archetype of the heroic deliverer. The problem of his marriage was resolved (at cost to all concerned) only after a difficult decision had been reached to submit concretely and literally to the power of the feminine by accepting an open liaison with Toni Wolff. Jung's involvement with his former patient, now his colleague, occurred with the full knowledge of his wife, whom he continued to love and honor. This still-controversial solution was never touted by the mature Jung as an example to others; rather it represented the best he could do against, and finally with, the power of the anima archetype, which he discovered by having to live it out. Toni Wolff helped Jung to see theoretically as well as personally that in the deep psyche the hero delivers himself from the mother archetype (and from the infantile unconsciousness that the hero's bondage to her authority represents for the conscious personality) only to encounter the demands of the anima. Like all mythic images, the anima is a root metaphor for an unconscious style of thought and behavior that underlies conscious choices. This archetype, usually symbolized by a woman closer in age to the man than his mother, but not invariably depicted as one figure, or even always as a woman, will become in her many guises his lifelong partner in the struggle for perspective, an indispensable source of the psychological complexities and ethical quandaries that will shape his consciousness and in no small measure his fate.

The anima was Jung's central discovery in the field of masculine psychology, for, as he learned, only the anima can deliver a man into a consciousness that is based, not on heroic self-mastery, but rather on empathic participation in life. Understanding the part of the psyche Jung called the anima is less an insight of the mind than an initiatory experience, a mystery to be lived until its core of meaningfulness for personality development is at last revealed. Jung solved the psychologist's problem, of formulating what can only be experienced, by resurrecting the ancient lore of initiation, with its rich symbolic descriptions of processes through which individuals get from one stage in life to another along a journey that begins with separation from the mother. The idea of initiation was the base from which Jung interpreted dreams and the progress of the psychological pilgrims with whom he worked analytically.

It was this discovery of initiation—the painful submission of the hero to the greater authority of archetypal forces with the power to mediate the development of consciousness—that marks Jung's mature understanding of masculine process and his radical departure from other depth psychologists of the modern era. As Jung's pupil (and analysand) Joseph Henderson was able to make clear in *Thresholds of Initiation,*[2] the hero role is an archetypal stage in the unconscious, denoting the formation of a strong ego-identity, which *precedes* the stage of the true initiate. This is a subtle point that Erik Erikson and other Freudian authors who have followed Jung's idea of "the stages of life" with their own models of ego development throughout the life-cycle seem to have missed. For Jung, as for no other psychological writer, the essence of genuine psychological development involves a giving up of the hero. When heroic consciousness dominates, one thinks one knows better than the unconscious who one is and feels one should therefore be in control of one's life. The hero is the mythologem of ego psychology and of the countless self-help books that keep appearing in this age of those who would "develop" the unconscious.

Obviously, the hero stage is a step forward for people at risk of drowning in the unconscious. The appearance of a hero in the unconscious of a young man who is not grounded enough to master such real-life heroic tasks as the completion of a college education or the overcoming of an addiction is a momentous event. Too often the archetypal basis of consciousness in youth is an unreal fantasy of greatness supplied by the *puer aeternus,* the god whose name means eternal boy. The shadow side of this archetype is the trickster, who seems to exist only to test psychosocial limits. These precursors of the hero archetype, as Henderson demonstrates in his book, are hard to disidentify with, and for many men in our culture their mastery is the work of the first half of life. It usually

[2] Joseph Henderson, *Thresholds of Initiation* (Middletown, Conn.: Wesleyan University Press, 1967).

requires educational experiences of the right kind to achieve the firm ego-grounding that the stage of the hero represents.

Among these educational experiences are the early love relationships described by Jung in "The Love Problem of a Student." Jung was ahead of his time in realizing that homosexual relationships, if the erotic expression is bounded by the faithfulness of the more mature person, can sometimes offer the right initiatory grounding at the preheroic stage. It is not clear, however, from his published writings whether he could see any value for individuation in love relationships between members of the same sex beyond this stage. A concretism in his understanding of the importance of the anima took hold here. Jung knew that the full psychological potential of being a man is possible only when the hero finally bows his own head and submits to initiation, not at the hands of an outer man or woman but according to the dictates of his own anima. Then a certain development of his eros from within (and not infrequently of his feeling for his place in the lives of others) will take place; so that he is at once better related to himself and to his fellow human beings. In Jung's own life, the development of the anima was intimately associated with events in his own heterosexual life. I have found, in the experience of my own practice, that while the stage of anima acceptance in men is almost always accompanied by an improvement in the quality and depth of relationships with women, the more or less permanent sexual orientation that appears at this time may be either homosexual or heterosexual, determined solely by the essential nature of the individual as mediated by the anima.

Acceptance of the anima is almost invariably difficult. The anima, as Jung points out, is the root word in animosity, and the anima (as moods) can be another name for resentment. Initiation by the anima means submitting to painful experiences of betrayal and disappointment when the projections she creates with her capacity for illusion fail to produce happiness. Accepting the pain of one's affects toward those experiences is a critical part of integrating the anima. Jung sometimes called the anima the "archetype of life," and he saw the individual as forced to suffer at the hands of life until life's power is sufficiently impressed upon him: the resultant conscious attitude, truly "a pearl of great price," is a sense of soul, which is also a respect for life's autonomy, the sort of wisdom personified by the Taoist sage Lao Tzu, whose name means "the old one." The wise old man stands behind the anima as an archetype of meaning, the masculine purpose and masculine result of this initiatory acceptance and integration of the feminine. Many contemporary analysts have questioned whether the anima may not also be an archetype that can mediate a woman's experience of herself. If so, the deep inner self revealed will be a feminine figure of wisdom, a personification of the goddess.

Jung was not ready to emphasize the anima for women. He felt that the women of his time had a special duty to realize their unconscious masculinity, which in his day was particularly in danger of being projected onto men. He understood the animus, only in some ways an analogue of the anima, to have its own particular character, as an archetype neither of life nor of meaning, but of spirit. Spirit was for Jung characteristically masculine, in contrast to soul, which he conceived as feminine. Even when he spoke of the animus as the women's soul-image, he meant that a woman has an unconscious masculine spirit where a man has an unconscious soul. Jung recognized that spirit and soul can figure in the development of both men and women, and he did speak of their *syzygy* or conjunction in the psyche of individuals. Nevertheless, with his women patients he concentrated on the recognition and integration of the spirit as their urgent psychological work. This therapeutic focus on the animus comes through clearly in what he says in the second selection from *Two Essays on Analytical Psychology* about the woman with a father transference to him and in his comments to his analysand and colleague Esther Harding as recorded in her personal notebook. When the spirit was an unconscious animus, projected onto men, he had to be freed up enough to function as an inner figure with whose help the woman could approach her own nature. Only then could she discriminate accurately who she was.

A man, by contrast, needed to learn with the help of a freed-up anima to relate to his nature with the right emotional attitude. Jung observed that among the men he saw, eros—defined as relatedness—tended to be more unconscious than in women. Logos—defined as discrimination—tended to be more unconscious in women. At times he went so far as to assert that eros was the woman's principle and logos the man's, which often sounds in our present cultural context like a sexist rigidity. Yet the unconscious vulnerability to eros in men and to logos in women seems to me to be a human fact, illustrating the everyday usefulness of Jung's gender psychology when applied to the area of his real expertise, the *unconscious* behavior of men and women. My own practice has taught me that, although neither women nor men have a monopoly on good judgment or good capacity for relationship, the unconscious of a woman reacts far more violently to opinions that threaten her world-concept while the unconscious of a man is more easily upset by feelings that violate his emotional equilibrium. Women seem, that is, to have a greater tolerance than men for feelings that challenge their prevailing patterns of relationship and men for ideas they disagree with. This notable difference seems to imply a more differentiated eros in women and a more differentiated logos in men.

On the other hand, Jung's idea of logos as the masculine principle and eros as the feminine principle has led to premature dogmatizing by some Jungian analysts as to the essential psychological character of men and of women and a storm of protest by other analysts, who have argued rightly for the complexity of individual experience. It is important to recognize that logos and eros are styles of consciousness available ultimately to both sexes, and that they represented opposites within Jung's own masculine nature. For (as the excerpts from the *Dream Analysis* seminar and Esther Harding's notebooks illustrate) it is precisely a masculine eros that anima development brings to consciousness in a man, and a feminine logos that animus development brings to a woman. In *Mysterium Coniunctionis*, Jung devoted far more space to his descriptions of the character of Sol and of Luna as personifications of these paradoxical opposites than to his earlier intuitive concepts of logos and eros. It is to this late masterwork that the reader should turn for a sense of Jung's mature thinking as to the nature of the psychological difference between men and women and between the masculine and feminine in both natures. A careful reading of that late work will enable one to dispense with the notion that Jung thought of the feminine as simply relatedness and the masculine as simply conscious discrimination. Indeed, there is a certain unrelatedness to the deep feminine spirit symbolized by Luna, with her dark cold moistness, that gives her a reflective depth; and there is an indiscriminate relatedness to Sol, with his bright warmth, that gives him a penetrating force.

In reading Jung's alchemical writings, one discovers the tradition into which his self-contradictory style of psychological explication falls. As others have observed, his is a hermetic style, one that conceals as much as it reveals, and expresses home truths in alchemical parables that seem to cancel out one another. Such a style is loyal only to nature. Jung's work on Western alchemy began to appear in print after he was sixty years old, and it is deeply grounded in the experience of masculine individuation after midlife. The process of incubating wisdom that the alchemical essays reflect and obliquely describe is one whose specific character and contents will be known only to those who are privy to the reflections of psychologically maturing individuals.

As he was putting his alchemical opus together, Jung gradually understood that even the masculine and feminine principles are not given; they are built up through experience, although the conditions for their creation follow archetypal laws. I have often observed that the building up of the feminine principle in a man during midlife obeys the following alchemical recipe, one that is only implied in Jung but is mentioned by other writers: salt conjoined with mercury produces Luna. Luna, the developed feminine principle, corresponds to an anima who is no longer naive; who has suffered enough (salt: bitterness, tears) and is capable of tricky ruthlessness in her own defense (mercury: trickster, the capacity to turn the tables on an aggressor). Men have the special task in midlife of making sure that Luna is well-enough integrated. (The brief excerpt from the difficult essay on salt speaks specifically to this inner work.) Luna is an initiated unconscious that is ready to interact with the initiated heroic consciousness that is Sol to produce an integration of personality. This is Jung's ultimate image of personality development, and it is obtained through his own masculine perspective.

"The Spirit Mercurius," source of the final selections in this volume, deserves special mention because it gives us our best glimpse into the archetypal ground of that perspective. This is probably the most personal of Jung's great essays on archetypes in that it is a description of Jung's own characteristic spirit and of the consciousness that governed the writing of his psychology. That Mercurius was for Jung the archetype of the unconscious tells us finally how masculine Jung's approach to the unconscious was. Despite his androgyny, Mercurius is a quintessentially masculine god, although not every masculinity will be grounded in this mythologem. So, not even this penetrating essay can be the last word on the masculine. Mercurius is, however, the archetype through which Jung came to understand his own psychological style. This piece stands among Jung's other writings like an ancient *herm*, an erect phallus placed by the Greeks at the gateways to new territories in honor of Hermes, who became the Roman Mercurius and the patron saint of alchemy. The phallic energy that was underground in Jung's childhood dream finds its way fully into the open with this essay. In the attributes of this god one can find Jung's own seminal ideas—the unconscious as an autonomous, creative being continually in motion between sets of opposites; the shifting shapes of the unconscious spirit as signals of its arrival at the gates of different gods; the trend of the unconscious toward stable wholeness within a contained intrapsychic life. Mercurius was the patron of Jung's alchemical effort at self-unification, Jung's ultimate father-figure and masculine way through the psyche. His is the restless masculine spirit that informs the contents of this volume.

John Beebe
San Francisco, September 1988

The editor would like to acknowledge the help of Cathie Brettschneider, Adam Frey, Joseph Henderson, Loren Hoekzema, John Levy, Daniel C. Noel, William McGuire, and Mary Webster.

ASPECTS OF THE MASCULINE

I. THE HERO*

THE ORIGIN OF THE HERO

251   The finest of all symbols of the libido is the human figure,
conceived as a demon or hero. Here the symbolism leaves the
objective, material realm of astral and meteorological images
and takes on human form, changing into a figure who passes
from joy to sorrow, from sorrow to joy, and, like the sun, now
stands high at the zenith and now is plunged into darkest night,
only to rise again in new splendour.[1] Just as the sun, by its own
motion and in accordance with its own inner law, climbs from
morn till noon, crosses the meridian and goes its downward way
towards evening, leaving its radiance behind it, and finally
plunges into all-enveloping night, so man sets his course by
immutable laws and, his journey over, sinks into darkness, to
rise again in his children and begin the cycle anew.

. . . .

297   The psychic life-force, the libido, symbolizes itself in the
sun [59] or personifies itself in figures of heroes with solar attributes. At the same time it expresses itself through phallic
symbols. Both possibilities are found on a late Babylonian gem
from Lajard's collection (fig. 19). In the middle stands an androgynous deity. On the masculine side there is a snake with
a sun halo round its head; on the feminine side another snake
with a sickle moon above it. This picture has a symbolic sexual
nuance: on the masculine side there is a lozenge, a favourite
symbol of the female genitals, and on the feminine side a wheel
without its rim. The spokes are thickened at the ends into

1 Hence the beautiful name of the sun-hero Gilgamesh, "The Man of Joy and
Sorrow," in Jensen, *Das Gilgamesch-Epos*.
59 Among the elements composing man, the Mithraic liturgy lays particular stress
on fire as the divine element, describing it as τὸ εἰς ἐμὴν κρᾶσιν θεοδώρητον (the
divine gift in my composition). Dieterich, *Mithrasliturgie*, p. 58.

    * [Ed. Note. Plates cited in the text from *Symbols of Transformation* have been omit-
ted.]

knobs, which, like the fingers we mentioned earlier, have a phallic meaning. It seems to be a phallic wheel such as was not unknown in antiquity. There are obscene gems on which Cupid is shown turning a wheel consisting entirely of phalli.[60] As to what the sun signifies, I discovered in the collection of antiquities at Verona a late Roman inscription with the following symbols: [61]

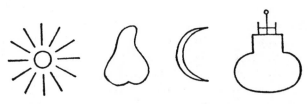

298   The symbolism is plain: sun = phallus, moon = vessel (uterus). This interpretation is confirmed by another monument from the same collection. The symbols are the same, except that the vessel [62] has been replaced by the figure of a woman. Certain symbols on coins can probably be interpreted in a similar manner. In Lajard's *Recherches sur la culte de Vénus* there is a coin from Perga, showing Artemis as a conical stone flanked by a masculine figure (alleged to be the deity Men) and a female figure (alleged to be Artemis). Men (otherwise called Lunus) appears on an Attic bas-relief with a spear, flanked by Pan with a club, and a female figure.[63] From this it is clear that sexuality as well as the sun can be used to symbolize the libido.

299   One further point deserves mention here. The dadophor Cautopates is often represented with a cock [64] and pine-cones. These are the attributes of the Phrygian god Men (pl. xxia), whose cult was very widespread. He was shown with the pileus [65] (or "Phrygian cap") and pine-cones, riding on the cock, and also

---

[60] An illustration of the periodicity or rhythm expressed in sexuality.

[61] Reproduced not from a photograph, but from a drawing I myself made.

[62] In a myth of the Bakairi Indians, of Brazil, a woman appears who sprang from a corn mortar. A Zulu myth tells a woman to catch a drop of blood in a pot, then close the pot, put it aside for eight months, and open it again in the ninth month. She follows this advice, opens the pot in the ninth month, and finds a child inside it. (Frobenius, I, p. 237.)

[63] Roscher, *Lexikon*, II, 2733/4, s.v. "Men."

[64] A well-known sun-animal.   [65] Like Mithras and the dadophors.

in the form of a boy, just as the dadophors were boyish figures. (This latter characteristic relates both them and Men to the Cabiri and Dactyls.) Now Men has affinities with Attis, the son and lover of Cybele. In Imperial times Men and Attis merged into one. Attis also wears the pileus like Men, Mithras, and the dadophors. As the son and lover of his mother he raises the incest problem. Incest leads logically to ritual castration in the Attis-Cybele cult; for according to legend the hero, driven mad by his mother, mutilates himself. I must refrain from going into

Fig. 19. Androgynous divinity
Late Babylonian gem

Fig. 20. Cybele and her son-lover Attis
Roman coin

this question more deeply at present, as I would prefer to discuss the incest problem at the end of this book. Here I would only point out that the incest motif is bound to arise, because when the regressing libido is introverted for internal or external reasons it always reactivates the parental imagos and thus apparently re-establishes the infantile relationship. But this relationship cannot be re-established, because the libido is an adult libido which is already bound to sexuality and inevitably imports an incompatible, incestuous character into the reactivated relationship to the parents.[66] It is this sexual character that now gives rise to the incest symbolism. Since incest must be avoided at all costs, the result is either the death of the son-lover or his self-castration as punishment for the incest he has

66 This explanation is not satisfactory, because I found it impossible to go into the archetypal incest problem and all its complications here. I have dealt with it at some length in my "Psychology of the Transference."

committed, or else the sacrifice of instinctuality, and especially of sexuality, as a means of preventing or expiating the incestuous longing. (Cf. fig. 20.) Sex being one of the most obvious examples of instinctuality, it is sex which is liable to be most affected by these sacrificial measures, i.e., through abstinence. The heroes are usually wanderers,[67] and wandering is a symbol of longing,[68] of the restless urge which never finds its object, of nostalgia for the lost mother. The sun comparison can easily be taken in this sense: the heroes are like the wandering sun, from which it is concluded that the myth of the hero is a solar myth. It seems to us, rather, that he is first and foremost a self-representation of the longing of the unconscious, of its unquenched and unquenchable desire for the light of consciousness. But consciousness, continually in danger of being led astray by its own light and of becoming a rootless will o' the wisp, longs for the healing power of nature, for the deep wells of being and for unconscious communion with life in all its countless forms. Here I must make way for the master, who has plumbed to the root of these Faustian longings:

> MEPHISTOPHELES: This lofty mystery I must now unfold.
> Goddesses throned in solitude, sublime,
> Set in no place, still less in any time,
> At the mere thought of them my blood runs cold.
> They are the Mothers!
> . . . .
> Goddesses, unknown to mortal mind,
> And named indeed with dread among our kind.
> To reach them you must plumb earth's deepest vault;
> That we have need of them is your own fault.

> FAUST: Where leads the way?

> MEPHISTOPHELES: There's none! To the untrodden,
> Untreadable regions—the unforgotten
> And unforgettable—for which prepare!
> There are no bolts, no hatches to be lifted,
> Through endless solitudes you shall be drifted.
> Can you imagine Nothing everywhere?
> . . . .

[67] Like Gilgamesh, Dionysus, Heracles, Mithras, etc.
[68] Cf. Graf, *Richard Wagner im Fliegenden Holländer.*

Supposing you had swum across the ocean
And gazed upon the immensity of space,
Still you would see wave after wave in motion,
And even though you feared the world should cease,
You'd still see something—in the limpid green
Of the calm deep are gliding dolphins seen,
The flying clouds above, sun, moon, and star.
But blank is that eternal Void afar.
You do not hear your footfall, and you meet
No solid ground on which to set your feet.

. . . .

Here, take this key.

. . . .

The key will smell the right place from all others:
Follow it down, it leads you to the Mothers.

. . . .

Then to the depths!—I could as well say height:
'It's all the same. From the Existent fleeing,
Take the free world of forms for your delight,
Rejoice in things that long have ceased from being.
The busy brood will weave like coiling cloud,
But swing your key to keep away the crowd!

. . . .

A fiery tripod warns you to beware,
This is the nethermost place where now you are.
You shall behold the Mothers by its light,
Some of them sit, some walk, some stand upright,
Just as they please. Formation, transformation,
Eternal Mind's eternal recreation.
Thronged round with images of things to be,
They see you not, shadows are all they see.
Then pluck up heart, the danger here is great,
Approach the tripod, do not hesitate,
And touch it with the key.[69]

69 Trans. based on MacNeice, pp. 175ff. Cf. also trans. by Wayne, Part II, pp. 76ff.

THE BATTLE FOR DELIVERANCE
FROM THE MOTHER

For Jung, the hero is a symbol of the developing ego's libido. By libido, Jung means not simply desire or psychological energy but psychological *purpose* as well. For him, the hero myth expresses the ego's desire to replace dependency upon the unconscious with self-direction—a purpose that necessitates an ambivalent struggle with the mother, who symbolizes the unconscious.

———————

441   Once again we recognize the typical elements of a libido myth: original bisexuality, immortality (invulnerability) through entry into the mother (splitting the mother with the foot), resurrection as a soul-bird, and production of fertility (rain). When a hero of this type causes his lance to be worshipped, he probably does so because he thinks it a valid equivalent of himself.

442   From this standpoint the passage in Job, which we quoted in Part I, appears in a new light:

> He hath set me up for his mark.
> His archers compass me round about,
> He cleaveth my reins asunder, and doth not spare;
> He poureth out my gall upon the ground.
> He breaketh me with breach upon breach,
> He runneth upon me like a giant.[50]

443   Here Job is voicing the torment of soul caused by the onslaught of unconscious desires; the libido festers in his flesh, a cruel God has overpowered him and pierced him through with barbed thoughts that agonize his whole being.

[50] Job 16: 12ff.

9

444   The same image occurs in Nietzsche:

> Stretched out, shivering,
> Like one half dead whose feet are warmed,
> Shaken by unknown fevers,
> Shuddering from the icy pointed arrows of frost,
> Hunted by thee, O thought,
> Unutterable! veiled! horrible one!
> Thou huntsman behind the clouds.
> Struck to the ground by thee,
> Thou mocking eye that gazeth at me from the dark:
> Thus do I lie,
> Twisting, writhing, tortured
> With eternal tortures,
> Smitten
> By thee, cruel huntsman,
> Thou unknown—God!
>
> Smite deeper!
> Smite once more!
> Pierce, rend my heart!
> What meaneth this torturing
> With blunt-toothed arrows?
> Why gazest thou again,
> Never weary of human agony,
> With sardonic gods'-eyes, flashing lightning?
> Why wilt thou not kill,
> Only torture, torture? [51]

445   No long-drawn explanations are needed to see in this comparison the martyred and sacrificed god whom we have already met in the Aztec crucifixions and in the sacrifice of Odin.[52] We meet the same image in depictions of the martyrdom of St. Sebastian, where the glowing, girlishly tender flesh of the young saint betrays all the pain of renunciation which the sensibility of the artist projected into it. An artist cannot prevent his work from being coloured by the psychology of his time. This is true in even higher degree of the Christian symbol, the Crucified pierced by the lance. It is a true symbol of the man of the Christian era, tormented by his desires and crucified in Christ.

[51] *Thus Spake Zarathustra.* (*Werke*, VI, pp. 367f.) [Cf. trans. by Common, p. 293.]
[52] Spielrein's patient said that she too had been shot by God three times—"then came a resurrection of the spirit."

446   That the torment which afflicts mankind does not come from
outside, but that man is his own huntsman, his own sacri-
ficer, his own sacrificial knife, is clear from another poem of
Nietzsche's, where the dualism is resolved into a psychic conflict
through the same symbolism:

> O Zarathustra,
> Most cruel Nimrod!
> Erstwhile hunter of God,
> Snare of all virtue,
> Arrow of evil!
> And now
> Self-hunted,
> Thine own quarry,
> Thyself pierced through . . .
>
> Now
> Alone with thyself,
> Split in thine own knowledge,
> Amidst a hundred mirrors
> To thine own self false,
> Amidst a hundred memories
> Uncertain,
> Languishing with each wound,
> Shivering with each frost,
> Strangled in thine own snares,
> Self-knower!
> Self-hangman!
>
> Why didst thou hang thyself
> With the noose of thy wisdom?
> Why hast thou enticed thyself
> Into the old serpent's Paradise?
> Why hast thou stolen
> Into thyself, thyself? [53]

447   The deadly arrows do not strike the hero from without;
it is himself who hunts, fights, and tortures himself. In him,
instinct wars with instinct; therefore the poet says, "Thyself
pierced through," which means that he is wounded by his own
arrow. As we know that the arrow is a libido-symbol, the mean-

[53] "Between Birds of Prey." (*Werke*, VIII, p. 414.) [Cf. trans. in *Ecce Homo and
Poetry* by Ludovici, Cohn, et al., p. 179.]

ing of this "piercing" is clear: it is the act of union with oneself, a sort of self-fertilization, and also a self-violation, a self-murder, so that Zarathustra can justly call himself his own hangman (like Odin, who sacrifices himself to Odin). One should not of course take this psychologem in too voluntaristic a sense: nobody deliberately inflicts such tortures on himself, they just happen to him. If a man reckons the unconscious as part of his personality, then one must admit that he is in fact raging against himself. But, in so far as the symbolism thrown up by his suffering is archetypal and collective, it can be taken as a sign that he is no longer suffering from himself, but rather from the spirit of the age. He is suffering from an objective, impersonal cause, from his collective unconscious which he has in common with all men.

448 Being wounded by one's own arrow signifies, therefore, a state of introversion. What this means we already know: the libido sinks "into its own depths" (a favourite image of Nietzsche's), and discovers in the darkness a substitute for the upper world it has abandoned—the world of memories ("Amidst a hundred memories"), the strongest and most influential of which are the earliest ones. It is the world of the child, the paradisal state of early infancy, from which we are driven out by the relentless law of time. In this subterranean kingdom slumber sweet feelings of home and the hopes of all that is to be. As Heinrich says of his miraculous work in Gerhart Hauptmann's *The Sunken Bell*:

> It sings a song, long lost and long forgotten,
> A song of home, a childlike song of love,
> Born in the waters of some fairy well,
> Known to all mortals, and yet heard of none.[54]

449 Yet "the danger is great," [55] as Mephistopheles says, for these depths fascinate. When the libido leaves the bright upper world, whether from choice, or from inertia, or from fate, it sinks back into its own depths, into the source from which it originally flowed, and returns to the point of cleavage, the navel, where it first entered the body. This point of cleavage is called the mother, because from her the current of life reached us. Whenever some great work is to be accomplished, before which a man

[54] Trans. by Meltzner, p. 75.   [55] *Faust*, Part II, "The Mothers."

recoils, doubtful of his strength, his libido streams back to the fountainhead—and that is the dangerous moment when the issue hangs between annihilation and new life. For if the libido gets stuck in the wonderland of this inner world,[56] then for the upper world man is nothing but a shadow, he is already moribund or at least seriously ill. But if the libido manages to tear itself loose and force its way up again, something like a miracle happens: the journey to the underworld was a plunge into the fountain of youth, and the libido, apparently dead, wakes to renewed fruitfulness. This idea is illustrated in an Indian myth: Vishnu sank into a profound trance, and in his slumber brought forth Brahma, who, enthroned on a lotus, rose out of Vishnu's navel, bringing with him the Vedas (pl. xlvia), which he diligently read. (Birth of creative thought from introversion.) But through Vishnu's ecstatic absentmindedness a mighty flood came upon the world. (Devouring and destruction of the world through introversion.) Taking advantage of the general confusion, a demon stole the Vedas and hid them in the depths. Brahma then roused Vishnu, who, changing himself into a fish (pl. xlvii), plunged into the flood, fought the demon, conquered him, and recaptured the Vedas.

450   This is a primitive way of describing the libido's entry into the interior world of the psyche, the unconscious. There, through its introversion and regression, contents are constellated which till now were latent. These are the primordial images, the archetypes, which have been so enriched with individual memories through the introversion of libido as to become perceptible to the conscious mind, in much the same way as the crystalline structure latent in the saturated solution takes visible shape from the aggregation of molecules. Since these introversions and regressions only occur at moments when a new orientation and a new adaptation are necessary, the constellated archetype is always the primordial image of the need of the

[56] This is mythologically represented in the legend of Theseus and Peirithous, who wanted to abduct Persephone from the underworld. They entered a chasm in the grove of Colonus and descended into the bowels of the earth. When they got down below they wished to rest a little, but found they had grown fast to the rocks and could not rise. In other words, they remained stuck in the mother and were lost to the upper world. Later Theseus was rescued by Heracles, who appeared in the role of the death-conquering hero. The Theseus myth is therefore a representation of the individuation process.

moment. Although the changing situations of life must appear infinitely various to our way of thinking, their possible number never exceeds certain natural limits; they fall into more or less typical patterns that repeat themselves over and over again. The archetypal structure of the unconscious corresponds to the average run of events. The changes that may befall a man are not infinitely variable; they are variations of certain typical occurrences which are limited in number. When therefore a distressing situation arises, the corresponding archetype will be constellated in the unconscious. Since this archetype is numinous, i.e., possesses a specific energy, it will attract to itself the contents of consciousness—conscious ideas that render it perceptible and hence capable of conscious realization. Its passing over into consciousness is felt as an illumination, a revelation, or a "saving idea." Repeated experience of this process has had the general result that, whenever a critical situation arises, the mechanism of introversion is made to function artificially by means of ritual actions which bring about a spiritual preparation, e.g., magical ceremonies, sacrifices, invocations, prayers, and suchlike. The aim of these ritual actions is to direct the libido towards the unconscious and compel it to introvert. If the libido connects with the unconscious, it is as though it were connecting with the mother, and this raises the incest-taboo. But as the unconscious is infinitely greater than the mother and is only symbolized by her, the fear of incest must be conquered if one is to gain possession of those "saving" contents—the treasure hard to attain. Since the son is not conscious of his incest tendency, it is projected upon the mother or her symbol. But the symbol of the mother is not the mother herself, so in reality there is not the slightest possibility of incest, and the taboo can therefore be ruled out as a reason for resistance. In so far as the mother represents the unconscious, the incest tendency, particularly when it appears as the amorous desire of the mother (e.g., Ishtar and Gilgamesh) or of the anima (e.g., Chryse and Philoctetes), is really only the desire of the unconscious to be taken notice of. The rejection of the unconscious usually has unfortunate results; its instinctive forces, if persistently disregarded, rise up in opposition: Chryse changes into a venomous serpent. The more negative the attitude of the conscious towards the unconscious, the more dangerous does the latter become.[57] Chryse's curse was fulfilled so completely that Philoctetes, on approaching her altar, wounded himself in the foot with his own poison-tipped arrow, or, according to other versions [58] which are in fact better attested, was bitten in the foot by a poisonous snake,[59] and fell into a decline.[60]

451   This very typical injury also destroyed Ra, and is described as follows in an Egyptian hymn:

The mouth of the god twitched with age,
So that he dropped his spittle on the earth,
And what he spat fell on the ground.
Isis then kneaded it with her hands
Together with the earth which was there;
She fashioned from it a noble worm
And made it like a spear.

[57] When the Greeks set out on their expedition to Troy, they wished, like the Argonauts and Heracles before them, to offer sacrifice on the altar of Chryse, a nymph who lived on an island of the same name, in order to secure a happy end to their voyage. Philoctetes was the only one among them who knew the way to her hidden shrine. But there the disaster befell him which is described above. Sophocles treats of this episode in his *Philoctetes*. We learn from a scholiast that Chryse offered the hero her love, but, on being scorned, cursed him. Philoctetes, like his forerunner Heracles, is the prototype of the wounded and ailing king, a motif that is continued in the legend of the Grail and in alchemical symbolism (cf. *Psychology and Alchemy*, pars. 491ff. and fig. 149).

[58] Roscher, *Lexikon*, 2318, 15ff., s.v. "Philoctetes."

[59] When the Russian sun-hero Oleg approached the skull of the slain horse, a snake darted out and bit him in the foot, so that he fell sick and died. And when Indra, in the form of Shyena the falcon, stole the soma drink, Krishanu the herdsman wounded him in the foot with an arrow. De Gubernatis, *Zoological Mythology*, II, pp. 181–82.

[60] Like the Grail king who guards the chalice, symbol of the mother. The myth of Philoctetes comes from the wider context of the Heracles cycle. Heracles had two mothers, the helpful Alcmene and the vengeful Hera, from whose breast he drank the milk of immortality. Heracles conquered Hera's serpents while yet in the cradle; that is, he freed himself from the grip of the unconscious. But from time to time Hera sent him fits of madness, in one of which he killed his own children. This is indirect proof that she was a lamia. According to one tradition, Heracles perpetrated this deed after refusing to perform the labours for his task-master Eurystheus. As a consequence of his hanging back, the libido that was ready for the work regressed to the unconscious mother-imago, and this resulted in madness. In this state he identified with the lamia and killed his own children. The Delphic oracle told him that he was named Heracles because he owed his immortal fame to Hera, who through her persecutions drove him to his great deeds. It is evident that the great deed really means overcoming the mother and thus winning immortality. His characteristic weapon, the club, he cut from the

She did not wind it living about her face,
But threw it in a coil upon the path
Upon which the great god was wont to walk
At pleasure through his two countries.
The noble god stepped forth in his splendour,
The gods who served Pharaoh accompanied him,
And he walked as he did each day.
Then the noble worm stung him . . .
The divine god opened his mouth,
And the voice of his majesty rang through the heavens.
And the gods cried: Behold! Behold!
He could not answer them,
His jawbones chattered,
All his limbs trembled,
And the poison invaded his flesh
As the Nile invades his territory.[61]

452   In this hymn Egypt has preserved for us a primitive version of
the snake-sting motif. The aging of the autumn sun as a symbol
of human senility is traced back to poisoning by a serpent. The
mother is blamed for causing the death of the sun-god with her
mischievous arts. The serpent symbolizes the mysterious numen
of the "mother" (and of other daimonia) who kills, but who
is at the same time man's only security against death, as she is
the source of life.[62] Accordingly, only the mother can cure him
who is sick unto death, and the hymn goes on to describe how
the gods were called together to take counsel:

Then came Isis with her wisdom,
Whose mouth is full of the breath of life,
Whose decree banishes pain,
And whose word gives life to those who no longer breathe.

maternal olive-tree. Like the sun, he possessed the arrows of Apollo. He conquered the Nemean lion in its cave, whose meaning is the "grave in the mother's
womb" (see the end of this chapter). Then follows the fight with the Hydra (cf.
also fig. 17) and his other deeds, which were all wished on him by Hera. All of
them symbolize the fight with the unconscious. At the end of his career, however,
he became the slave of Omphale ($\dot{o}\mu\phi a\lambda\dot{o}s$ = 'navel') as the oracle prophesied:
that is, he had to submit after all to the unconscious.
61 This and the following passages trans. from Erman, pp. 265–67, modified.
62 How concretely this mythologem is taken on the primitive level can be seen
from the description in Gatti, South of the Sahara (pp. 226ff.), of a medicine-
woman in Natal who had a twenty-foot boa constrictor as her familiar.

She said: What is it, what is it, divine Father?
Behold, a worm hath done thee this wrong.

Tell me thy name, divine Father,
For he whose name is spoken shall live.

453   Ra answers:

I am he who created heaven and earth, and piled up the mountains,
And made all living things.
I am he who made the water and caused the great flood,
Who made the Bull of his Mother,
Who is the Begetter.

The poison did not depart, it went further,
The great god was not healed.
Then said Isis to Ra:
That is not thy name which thou tellest me.
Tell me thy name, that the poison may depart,
For he whose name is spoken shall live.

454   Finally Ra decides to utter his true name. He was only par-
tially cured, just as Osiris was only incompletely reconstituted,
and in addition he lost his power and finally had to retire on
the back of the heavenly cow.

455   The poisonous worm is a deadly instead of an animating
form of libido. The "true name" is Ra's soul and magic power
(his libido). What Isis demands is the transference of libido to
the mother. This request is fulfilled to the letter, for the aging
god returns to the heavenly cow, the symbol of the mother.

456   The meaning of this symbolism becomes clear in the light of
what we said earlier: the forward-striving libido which rules the
conscious mind of the son demands separation from the mother,
but his childish longing for her prevents this by setting up a
psychic resistance that manifests itself in all kinds of neurotic
fears—that is to say, in a general fear of life. The more a person
shrinks from adapting himself to reality, the greater becomes
the fear which increasingly besets his path at every point. Thus
a vicious circle is formed: fear of life and people causes more
shrinking back, and this in turn leads to infantilism and finally
"into the mother." The reasons for this are generally projected
outside oneself: the fault lies with external circumstances, or
else the parents are made responsible. And indeed, it remains

17

to be found out how much the mother is to blame for not letting the son go. The son will naturally try to explain everything by the wrong attitude of the mother, but he would do better to refrain from all such futile attempts to excuse his own ineptitude by laying the blame on his parents.

457   This fear of life is not just an imaginary bogy, but a very real panic, which seems disproportionate only because its real source is unconscious and therefore projected: the young, growing part of the personality, if prevented from living or kept in check, generates fear and changes into fear. The fear seems to come from the mother, but actually it is the deadly fear of the instinctive, unconscious, inner man who is cut off from life by the continual shrinking back from reality. If the mother is felt as the obstacle, she then becomes the vengeful pursuer. Naturally it is not the real mother, although she too may seriously injure her child by the morbid tenderness with which she pursues it into adult life, thus prolonging the infantile attitude beyond the proper time. It is rather the mother-imago that has turned into a lamia.[63] (Cf. pls. xxxviii*a*, xlviii.) The mother-imago, however, represents the unconscious, and it is as much a vital necessity for the unconscious to be joined to the conscious as it is for the latter not to lose contact with the unconscious. Nothing endangers this connection more in a man than a successful life; it makes him forget his dependence on the unconscious. The case of Gilgamesh is instructive in this respect: he was so successful that the gods, the representatives of the unconscious, saw themselves compelled to deliberate how they could best bring about his downfall. Their efforts were unavailing at first, but when the hero had won the herb of immortality (cf. pl. xix) and was almost at his goal, a serpent stole the elixir of life from him while he slept.

458   The demands of the unconscious act at first like a paralysing poison on a man's energy and resourcefulness, so that it may well be compared to the bite of a poisonous snake. (Cf. fig. 30.)

---

[63] The myth of Hippolytus has similar ingredients: His step-mother Phaedra falls in love with him, he repulses her, she accuses him of violation before her husband, who calls upon Poseidon to punish Hippolytus. Whereupon a monster comes out of the sea; Hippolytus' horses take fright and drag him to death. But he is restored to life by Aesculapius, and the gods convey him to the grove of the wise nymph Egeria, the counsellor of Numa Pompilius.

Apparently it is a hostile demon who robs him of energy, but in actual fact it is his own unconscious whose alien tendencies are beginning to check the forward striving of the

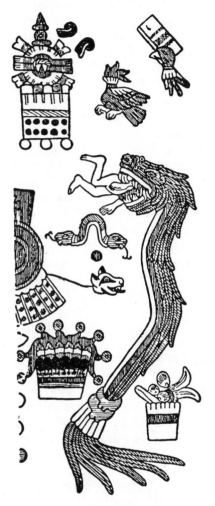

Fig. 30. Quetzalcoatl devouring a man
From the Codex Borbonicus, Aztec 16th century

conscious mind. The cause of this process is often extremely obscure, the more so as it is complicated by all kinds of external factors and subsidiary causes, such as difficulties in work, disappointments, failures, reduced efficiency due to age, depressing family problems, and so on and so forth. According to the myths it is the woman who secretly enslaves a man, so that he can no longer free himself from her and becomes a child again.[64] It is also significant that Isis, the sister-wife of the sun-god, creates the poisonous serpent from his spittle, which, like all bodily secretions, has a magical significance, being a libido equivalent. She creates the serpent from the libido of the god, and by this means weakens him and makes him dependent on her. Delilah acts in the same way with Samson: by cutting off his hair, the sun's rays, she robs him of his strength. This demon-woman of mythology is in truth the "sister-wife-mother," the woman in the man, who unexpectedly turns up during the second half of life and tries to effect a forcible change of personality. I have dealt with certain aspects of this change in my essay on "The Stages of Life." It consists in a partial feminization of the man and a corresponding masculinization of the woman. Often it takes place under very dramatic circumstances: the man's strongest quality, his Logos principle, turns against him and as it were betrays him. The same thing happens with the Eros of the woman. The man becomes rigidly set in his previous attitude, while the woman remains caught in her emotional ties and fails to develop her reason and understanding, whose place is then taken by equally obstinate and inept "animus" opinions. The fossilization of the man shrouds itself in a smoke-screen of moods, ridiculous irritability, feelings of distrust and resentment, which are meant to justify his rigid attitude. A perfect example of this type of psychology is Schreber's account of his own psychosis, *Memoirs of My Nervous Illness.*[65]

459   The paralysis of progressive energy has in truth some very disagreeable aspects. It seems like an unwelcome accident or a positive catastrophe, which one would naturally rather avoid. In most cases the conscious personality rises up against the assault of the unconscious and resists its demands, which, it is clearly felt, are directed not only against all the weak spots in the man's character, but also against his chief virtue (the differentiated function and the ideal). It is evident from the myths of Heracles and Gilgamesh that this assault can become the

---

[64] Cf. Heracles and Omphale.
[65] The case was written up at the time by Freud in a very unsatisfactory way after I had drawn his attention to the book. See "Psycho-Analytical Notes upon an Autobiographical Account of a Case of Paranoia."

source of energy for an heroic conflict; indeed, so obvious is this impression that one has to ask oneself whether the apparent enmity of the maternal archetype is not a ruse on the part of Mater Natura for spurring on her favoured child to his highest achievement. The vengeful Hera would then appear as the stern "Mistress Soul," who imposes the most difficult labours on her hero and threatens him with destruction unless he plucks up courage for the supreme deed and actually becomes what he always potentially was. The hero's victory over the "mother," or over her daemonic representative (dragon, etc.), is never anything but temporary. What must be regarded as regression in a young person—feminization of the man (partial identity with the mother) and masculinization of the woman (partial identity with the father)—acquires a different meaning in the second half of life. The assimilation of contrasexual tendencies then becomes a task that must be fulfilled in order to keep the libido in a state of progression. The task consists in integrating the unconscious, in bringing together "conscious" and "unconscious." I have called this the individuation process, and for further details must refer the reader to my later works.[65a] At this stage the mother-symbol no longer connects back to the beginnings, but points towards the unconscious as the creative matrix of the future. "Entry into the mother" then means establishing a relationship between the ego and the unconscious. Nietzsche probably means something of the kind in his poem:

> Why hast thou enticed thyself
> Into the old serpent's Paradise?
> Why hast thou stolen
> Into thyself, thyself?
>
> A sick man now,
> Sick of the serpent's poison; [66]
> A captive now
> Who drew the hardest lot:
> Bent double
> Working in thine own pit,

[65a] [Cf. especially "A Study in the Process of Individuation."—EDITORS.]

[66] Spielrein's patient was also sick from "snake poison" (p. 385). Schreber said he was infected by "corpse poison," that "soul murder" had been committed on him, etc. (pp. 54ff.).

> Encaved within thyself,
> Burrowing into thyself,
> Heavy-handed,
> Stiff,
> A corpse—
> Piled with a hundred burdens,
> Loaded to death with thyself,
> A knower!
> Self-knower!
> The wise Zarathustra!
> You sought the heaviest burden
> And found yourself.[67]

460   Sunk in his own depths, he is like one buried in the earth; a dead man who has crawled back into the mother; [68] a Kaineus "piled with a hundred burdens" and pressed down to death, groaning beneath the intolerable weight of his own self and his own destiny. Who does not think here of Mithras, who, in the Taurophoria, took his bull (or, as the Egyptian hymn says, "the bull of his mother"), namely his love for his Mater Natura, on his back, and with this heaviest burden set forth on the *via dolorosa* of the Transitus? [69] The way of this passion leads to the cave in which the bull is sacrificed. So, too, Christ had to bear the Cross [70] to the place of sacrifice, where, according to the Christian version, the Lamb was slain in the form of the

67 "Between Birds of Prey." (*Werke*, VIII, p. 414.) [Cf. trans. in *Ecce Homo and Poetry*, by Ludovici et al., p. 179.]

68 Spielrein's patient (p. 336) uses the same images; she speaks of the "rigidity of the soul on the cross," of "stone figures" who must be "melted."

69 Gurlitt says: "The carrying of the bull [pl. XLIXa] is one of the difficult ἔθλα which Mithras performed for the redemption of mankind; it corresponds roughly —if we may compare small things with great—to Christ carrying the cross." ("Vorbericht über Ausgrabungen in Pettau"; cited in Cumont, *Textes*, I, p. 172.)

70 Robertson (*Christianity and Mythology*, p. 401) makes an interesting contribution to the symbol of carrying the cross: Samson carried the gate-posts of the city of Gaza, and died between the pillars of the temple of the Philistines. Heracles carried his pillars to Gades (Cadiz), where, according to the Syrian version of the legend, he died. The Pillars of Hercules mark the point in the west where the sun sinks into the sea. "In ancient art," says Robertson, "he was actually represented carrying the two pillars in such a way under his arms that they form exactly a cross. Here, probably, we have the origin of the myth of Jesus carrying his own cross to the place of execution. Singularly enough, the three Synoptics substitute for Jesus as cross-bearer one Simon, a man of Cyrene. Cyrene is in Libya, the legendary scene, as we saw, of the pillar-carrying exploit of Heracles;

god, and was then laid to earth in the sepulchre.[71] The cross, or whatever other heavy burden the hero carries, is *himself*, or rather *the* self, his wholeness, which is both God and animal—not merely the empirical man, but the totality of his being, which is rooted in his animal nature and reaches out beyond the merely human towards the divine. His wholeness implies a tremendous tension of opposites paradoxically at one with themselves, as in the cross, their most perfect symbol. What seems like a poetic figure of speech in Nietzsche is really an age-old myth. It is as if the poet could still sense, beneath the words of contemporary speech and in the images that crowd in upon his imagination, the ghostly presence of bygone spiritual worlds, and possessed the capacity to make them come alive again. As Gerhart Hauptmann says: "Poetry is the art of letting the primordial word resound through the common word." [72]

---

and Simon (Simeon) is the nearest Greek name-form to Samson. . . . In Palestine, Simon, or Sem, was actually a god-name, representing the ancient sun-god Shemesh, identified with Baal, from whose mythus that of Samson unquestionably arose; and the God Simon was especially worshipped in Samaria." I give Robertson's words here, but must emphasize that the etymological connection between Simon and Samson is exceedingly questionable. The cross of Heracles may well be the sun-wheel, for which the Greeks used the symbol of the cross. The sun-wheel on the bas-relief of the Little Metropolis in Athens actually contains a cross which looks very like the Maltese cross. (Cf. Thiele, *Antike Himmelsbilder*, p. 59.) Here I must refer the reader to the mandala symbolism in *Psychology and Alchemy* and in *The Secret of the Golden Flower*.

71 The legend of Ixion (pl. XLVI*b*), who was "crucified on the four-spoked wheel" (Pindar), says the same thing. Ixion first murdered his father-in-law but was afterwards absolved from guilt by Zeus and blessed with his favour. Ixion, with gross ingratitude, then tried to seduce Hera, but Zeus tricked him by getting the cloud-goddess Nephele to assume Hera's shape. From this union the centaurs are said to have sprung. Ixion boasted of his deed, but as a punishment for his crimes Zeus cast him into the underworld, where he was bound on a wheel that turned forever in the wind.

72 Cited from the *Zentralblatt für Psychoanalyse*, II (1912), p. 365 [in a note by W. Stekel, quoting extracts from Hauptmann's published diary.—EDITORS].

II. INITIATION AND THE
DEVELOPMENT OF MASCULINITY

THE STAGES OF LIFE

Jung's notion of the stages of life implies a lifelong series of initiations. The developing individual struggles successively with problems typical of each time of life, and these problems are never fully solved. Rather, they serve the purpose of promoting consciousness. When Jung conceives this development in masculine, transcendental terms as fulfillment of an inner demand for the progress of consciousness, he continues the German Romantic tradition of Schopenhauer and Nietzsche. Schopenhauer had postulated a *principium individuationis*, which Jung reads as the psychological drive to be the self that one truly is. Nietzsche supplied the idea of the life-task, which in Jung becomes the moral imperative to accomplish one's mission of individuation. Yet Jung sees clearly that genuine development will force the individual to give up all pretensions to heroic mastery. Using the metaphor of the sun's daily journey, he envisioned the psychology of the individual as an ascent to bright consciousness in the first half of life, followed by a sacrifice of that brightness in a descent to the unconscious in life's second half. In a man, this loss of ego was compensated by the emergence of the anima.

---

759   And here we come to our real theme—the problem of the stages of life. First of all we must deal with the period of youth. It extends roughly from the years just after puberty to middle life, which itself begins between the thirty-fifth and fortieth year.

760   I might well be asked why I begin with the second stage, as though there were no problems connected with childhood. The

complex psychic life of the child is, of course, a problem of the first magnitude to parents, educators, and doctors, but when normal the child has no real problems of its own. It is only the adult human being who can have doubts about himself and be at variance with himself.

761   We are all familiar with the sources of the problems that arise in the period of youth. For most people it is the demands of life which harshly put an end to the dream of childhood. If the individual is sufficiently well prepared, the transition to a profession or career can take place smoothly. But if he clings to illusions that are contrary to reality, then problems will surely arise. No one can take the step into life without making certain assumptions, and occasionally these assumptions are false—that is, they do not fit the conditions into which one is thrown. Often it is a question of exaggerated expectations, underestimation of difficulties, unjustified optimism, or a negative attitude. One could compile quite a list of the false assumptions that give rise to the first conscious problems.

762   But it is not always the contradiction between subjective assumptions and external facts that gives rise to problems; it may just as often be inner, psychic difficulties. They may exist even when things run smoothly in the outside world. Very often it is the disturbance of psychic equilibrium caused by the sexual instinct; equally often it is the feeling of inferiority which springs from an unbearable sensitivity. These inner conflicts may exist even when adaptation to the outer world has been achieved without apparent effort. It even seems as if young people who have had a hard struggle for existence are spared inner problems, while those who for some reason or other have no difficulty with adaptation run into problems of sex or conflicts arising from a sense of inferiority.

763   People whose own temperaments offer problems are often neurotic, but it would be a serious misunderstanding to confuse the existence of problems with neurosis. There is a marked difference between the two in that the neurotic is ill because he is unconscious of his problems, while the person with a difficult temperament suffers from his conscious problems without being ill.

764   If we try to extract the common and essential factors from the almost inexhaustible variety of individual problems found

in the period of youth, we meet in all cases with one particular feature: a more or less patent clinging to the childhood level of consciousness, a resistance to the fateful forces in and around us which would involve us in the world. Something in us wishes to remain a child, to be unconscious or, at most, conscious only of the ego; to reject everything strange, or else subject it to our will; to do nothing, or else indulge our own craving for pleasure or power. In all this there is something of the inertia of matter; it is a persistence in the previous state whose range of consciousness is smaller, narrower, and more egoistic than that of the dualistic phase. For here the individual is faced with the necessity of recognizing and accepting what is different and strange as a part of his own life, as a kind of "also-I."

765   The essential feature of the dualistic phase is the widening of the horizon of life, and it is this that is so vigorously resisted. To be sure, this expansion—or diastole, as Goethe called it—had started long before this. It begins at birth, when the child abandons the narrow confinement of the mother's body; and from then on it steadily increases until it reaches a climax in the problematical state, when the individual begins to struggle against it.

766   What would happen to him if he simply changed himself into that foreign-seeming "also-I" and allowed the earlier ego to vanish into the past? We might suppose this to be a quite practical course. The very aim of religious education, from the exhortation to put off the old Adam right back to the rebirth rituals of primitive races, is to transform the human being into the new, future man, and to allow the old to die away.

767   Psychology teaches us that, in a certain sense, there is nothing in the psyche that is old; nothing that can really, finally die away. Even Paul was left with a thorn in the flesh. Whoever protects himself against what is new and strange and regresses to the past falls into the same neurotic condition as the man who identifies himself with the new and runs away from the past. The only difference is that the one has estranged himself from the past and the other from the future. In principle both are doing the same thing: they are reinforcing their narrow range of consciousness instead of shattering it in the tension of opposites and building up a state of wider and higher consciousness.

27

768   This outcome would be ideal if it could be brought about in the second stage of life—but there's the rub. For one thing, nature cares nothing whatsoever about a higher level of consciousness; quite the contrary. And then society does not value these feats of the psyche very highly; its prizes are always given for achievement and not for personality, the latter being rewarded for the most part posthumously. These facts compel us towards a particular solution: we are forced to limit ourselves to the attainable, and to differentiate particular aptitudes in which the socially effective individual discovers his true self.

769   Achievement, usefulness and so forth are the ideals that seem to point the way out of the confusions of the problematical state. They are the lodestars that guide us in the adventure of broadening and consolidating our physical existence; they help us to strike our roots in the world, but they cannot guide us in the development of that wider consciousness to which we give the name of culture. In the period of youth, however, this course is the normal one and in all circumstances preferable to merely tossing about in a welter of problems.

770   The dilemma is often solved, therefore, in this way: whatever is given to us by the past is adapted to the possibilities and demands of the future. We limit ourselves to the attainable, and this means renouncing all our other psychic potentialities. One man loses a valuable piece of his past, another a valuable piece of his future. Everyone can call to mind friends or schoolmates who were promising and idealistic youngsters, but who, when we meet them again years later, seem to have grown dry and cramped in a narrow mould. These are examples of the solution mentioned above.

771   The serious problems in life, however, are never fully solved. If ever they should appear to be so it is a sure sign that something has been lost. The meaning and purpose of a problem seem to lie not in its solution but in our working at it incessantly. This alone preserves us from stultification and petrifaction. So also the solution of the problems of youth by restricting ourselves to the attainable is only temporarily valid and not lasting in a deeper sense. Of course, to win for oneself a place in society and to transform one's nature so that it is more or less fitted to this kind of existence is in all cases a considerable achievement. It is a fight waged within oneself as well as out-

side, comparable to the struggle of the child for an ego. That struggle is for the most part unobserved because it happens in the dark; but when we see how stubbornly childish illusions and assumptions and egoistic habits are still clung to in later years we can gain some idea of the energies that were needed to form them. And so it is with the ideals, convictions, guiding ideas and attitudes which in the period of youth lead us out into life, for which we struggle, suffer, and win victories: they grow together with our own being, we apparently change into them, we seek to perpetuate them indefinitely and as a matter of course, just as the young person asserts his ego in spite of the world and often in spite of himself.

772   The nearer we approach to the middle of life, and the better we have succeeded in entrenching ourselves in our personal attitudes and social positions, the more it appears as if we had discovered the right course and the right ideals and principles of behaviour. For this reason we suppose them to be eternally valid, and make a virtue of unchangeably clinging to them. We overlook the essential fact that the social goal is attained only at the cost of a diminution of personality. Many—far too many— aspects of life which should also have been experienced lie in the lumber-room among dusty memories; but sometimes, too, they are glowing coals under grey ashes.

773   Statistics show a rise in the frequency of mental depressions in men about forty. In women the neurotic difficulties generally begin somewhat earlier. We see that in this phase of life—between thirty-five and forty—an important change in the human psyche is in preparation. At first it is not a conscious and striking change; it is rather a matter of indirect signs of a change which seems to take its rise in the unconscious. Often it is something like a slow change in a person's character; in another case certain traits may come to light which had disappeared since childhood; or again, one's previous inclinations and interests begin to weaken and others take their place. Conversely —and this happens very frequently—one's cherished convictions and principles, especially the moral ones, begin to harden and to grow increasingly rigid until, somewhere around the age of fifty, a period of intolerance and fanaticism is reached. It is as if the existence of these principles were endangered and it were therefore necessary to emphasize them all the more.

774   The wine of youth does not always clear with advancing years; sometimes it grows turbid. All the phenomena mentioned above can best be seen in rather one-sided people, turning up sometimes sooner and sometimes later. Their appearance, it seems to me, is often delayed by the fact that the parents of the person in question are still alive. It is then as if the period of youth were being unduly drawn out. I have seen this especially in the case of men whose fathers were long-lived. The death of the father then has the effect of a precipitate and almost catastrophic ripening.

775   I know of a pious man who was a churchwarden and who, from the age of forty onward, showed a growing and finally unbearable intolerance in matters of morality and religion. At the same time his moods grew visibly worse. At last he was nothing more than a darkly lowering pillar of the Church. In this way he got along until the age of fifty-five, when suddenly, sitting up in bed in the middle of the night, he said to his wife: "Now at last I've got it! I'm just a plain rascal." Nor did this realization remain without results. He spent his declining years in riotous living and squandered a goodly part of his fortune. Obviously quite a likable fellow, capable of both extremes!

776   The very frequent neurotic disturbances of adult years all have one thing in common: they want to carry the psychology of the youthful phase over the threshold of the so-called years of discretion. Who does not know those touching old gentlemen who must always warm up the dish of their student days, who can fan the flame of life only by reminiscences of their heroic youth, but who, for the rest, are stuck in a hopelessly wooden Philistinism? As a rule, to be sure, they have this one merit which it would be wrong to undervalue: they are not neurotic, but only boring and stereotyped. The neurotic is rather a person who can never have things as he would like them in the present, and who can therefore never enjoy the past either.

777   As formerly the neurotic could not escape from childhood, so now he cannot part with his youth. He shrinks from the grey thoughts of approaching age, and, feeling the prospect before him unbearable, is always straining to look behind him. Just as the childish person shrinks back from the unknown in the world and in human existence, so the grown man shrinks back from the second half of life. It is as if unknown and dangerous tasks

awaited him, or as if he were threatened with sacrifices and losses which he does not wish to accept, or as if his life up to now seemed to him so fair and precious that he could not relinquish it.

778   Is it perhaps at bottom the fear of death? That does not seem to me very probable, because as a rule death is still far in the distance and therefore somewhat abstract. Experience shows us, rather, that the basic cause of all the difficulties of this transition is to be found in a deep-seated and peculiar change within the psyche. In order to characterize it I must take for comparison the daily course of the sun—but a sun that is endowed with human feeling and man's limited consciousness. In the morning it rises from the nocturnal sea of unconsciousness and looks upon the wide, bright world which lies before it in an expanse that steadily widens the higher it climbs in the firmament. In this extension of its field of action caused by its own rising, the sun will discover its significance; it will see the attainment of the greatest possible height, and the widest possible dissemination of its blessings, as its goal. In this conviction the sun pursues its course to the unforeseen zenith—unforeseen, because its career is unique and individual, and the culminating point could not be calculated in advance. At the stroke of noon the descent begins. And the descent means the reversal of all the ideals and values that were cherished in the morning. The sun falls into contradiction with itself. It is as though it should draw in its rays instead of emitting them. Light and warmth decline and are at last extinguished.

779   All comparisons are lame, but this simile is at least not lamer than others. A French aphorism sums it up with cynical resignation: *Si jeunesse savait, si vieillesse pouvait.*

780   Fortunately we are not rising and setting suns, for then it would fare badly with our cultural values. But there is something sunlike within us, and to speak of the morning and spring, of the evening and autumn of life is not mere sentimental jargon. We thus give expression to psychological truths and, even more, to physiological facts, for the reversal of the sun at noon changes even bodily characteristics. Especially among southern races one can observe that older women develop deep, rough voices, incipient moustaches, rather hard features and other masculine traits. On the other hand the masculine physique is

31

toned down by feminine features, such as adiposity and softer facial expressions.

781   There is an interesting report in the ethnological literature about an Indian warrior chief to whom in middle life the Great Spirit appeared in a dream. The spirit announced to him that from then on he must sit among the women and children, wear women's clothes, and eat the food of women. He obeyed the dream without suffering a loss of prestige. This vision is a true expression of the psychic revolution of life's noon, of the beginning of life's decline. Man's values, and even his body, do tend to change into their opposites.

782   We might compare masculinity and femininity and their psychic components to a definite store of substances of which, in the first half of life, unequal use is made. A man consumes his large supply of masculine substance and has left over only the smaller amount of feminine substance, which must now be put to use. Conversely, the woman allows her hitherto unused supply of masculinity to become active.

783   This change is even more noticeable in the psychic realm than in the physical. How often it happens that a man of forty-five or fifty winds up his business, and the wife then dons the trousers and opens a little shop where he perhaps performs the duties of a handyman. There are many women who only awaken to social responsibility and to social consciousness after their fortieth year. In modern business life, especially in America, nervous breakdowns in the forties are a very common occurrence. If one examines the victims one finds that what has broken down is the masculine style of life which held the field up to now, and that what is left over is an effeminate man. Contrariwise, one can observe women in these self-same business spheres who have developed in the second half of life an uncommonly masculine tough-mindedness which thrusts the feelings and the heart aside. Very often these changes are accompanied by all sorts of catastrophes in marriage, for it is not hard to imagine what will happen when the husband discovers his tender feelings and the wife her sharpness of mind.

784   The worst of it all is that intelligent and cultivated people live their lives without even knowing of the possibility of such transformations. Wholly unprepared, they embark upon the second half of life. Or are there perhaps colleges for forty-year-

olds which prepare them for their coming life and its demands as the ordinary colleges introduce our young people to a knowledge of the world? No, thoroughly unprepared we take the step into the afternoon of life; worse still, we take this step with the false assumption that our truths and ideals will serve us as hitherto. But we cannot live the afternoon of life according to the programme of life's morning; for what was great in the morning will be little at evening, and what in the morning was true will at evening have become a lie. I have given psychological treatment to too many people of advancing years, and have looked too often into the secret chambers of their souls, not to be moved by this fundamental truth.

785   Ageing people should know that their lives are not mounting and expanding, but that an inexorable inner process enforces the contraction of life. For a young person it is almost a sin, or at least a danger, to be too preoccupied with himself; but for the ageing person it is a duty and a necessity to devote serious attention to himself. After having lavished its light upon the world, the sun withdraws its rays in order to illuminate itself. Instead of doing likewise, many old people prefer to be hypochondriacs, niggards, pedants, applauders of the past or else eternal adolescents—all lamentable substitutes for the illumination of the self, but inevitable consequences of the delusion that the second half of life must be governed by the principles of the first.

786   I said just now that we have no schools for forty-year-olds. That is not quite true. Our religions were always such schools in the past, but how many people regard them like that today? How many of us older ones have been brought up in such a school and really prepared for the second half of life, for old age, death and eternity?

787   A human being would certainly not grow to be seventy or eighty years old if this longevity had no meaning for the species. The afternoon of human life must also have a significance of its own and cannot be merely a pitiful appendage to life's morning. The significance of the morning undoubtedly lies in the development of the individual, our entrenchment in the outer world, the propagation of our kind, and the care of our children. This is the obvious purpose of nature. But when this purpose has been attained—and more than attained—shall the

33

earning of money, the extension of conquests, and the expansion of life go steadily on beyond the bounds of all reason and sense? Whoever carries over into the afternoon the law of the morning, or the natural aim, must pay for it with damage to his soul, just as surely as a growing youth who tries to carry over his childish egoism into adult life must pay for this mistake with social failure. Money-making, social achievement, family and posterity are nothing but plain nature, not culture. Culture lies outside the purpose of nature. Could by any chance culture be the meaning and purpose of the second half of life?

788   In primitive tribes we observe that the old people are almost always the guardians of the mysteries and the laws, and it is in these that the cultural heritage of the tribe is expressed. How does the matter stand with us? Where is the wisdom of our old people, where are their precious secrets and their visions? For the most part our old people try to compete with the young. In the United States it is almost an ideal for a father to be the brother of his sons, and for the mother to be if possible the younger sister of her daughter.

789   I do not know how much of this confusion is a reaction against an earlier exaggeration of the dignity of age, and how much is to be charged to false ideals. These undoubtedly exist, and the goal of those who hold them lies behind, and not ahead. Therefore they are always striving to turn back. We have to grant these people that it is hard to see what other goal the second half of life can offer than the well-known aims of the first. Expansion of life, usefulness, efficiency, the cutting of a figure in society, the shrewd steering of offspring into suitable marriages and good positions—are not these purposes enough? Unfortunately not enough meaning and purpose for those who see in the approach of old age a mere diminution of life and can feel their earlier ideals only as something faded and worn out. Of course, if these persons had filled up the beaker of life earlier and emptied it to the lees, they would feel quite differently about everything now; they would have kept nothing back, everything that wanted to catch fire would have been consumed, and the quiet of old age would be very welcome to them. But we must not forget that only a very few people are artists in life; that the art of life is the most distinguished and rarest of all the arts. Who ever succeeded in draining the whole cup with grace?

So for many people all too much unlived life remains over—sometimes potentialities which they could never have lived with the best of wills, so that they approach the threshold of old age with unsatisfied demands which inevitably turn their glances backward.

790   It is particularly fatal for such people to look back. For them a prospect and a goal in the future are absolutely necessary. That is why all great religions hold out the promise of a life beyond, of a supramundane goal which makes it possible for mortal man to live the second half of life with as much purpose and aim as the first. For the man of today the expansion of life and its culmination are plausible goals, but the idea of life after death seems to him questionable or beyond belief. Life's cessation, that is, death, can only be accepted as a reasonable goal either when existence is so wretched that we are only too glad for it to end, or when we are convinced that the sun strives to its setting "to illuminate distant races" with the same logical consistency it showed in rising to the zenith. But to believe has become such a difficult art today that it is beyond the capacity of most people, particularly the educated part of humanity. They have become too accustomed to the thought that, with regard to immortality and such questions, there are innumerable contradictory opinions and no convincing proofs. And since "science" is the catchword that seems to carry the weight of absolute conviction in the temporary world, we ask for "scientific" proofs. But educated people who can think know very well that proof of this kind is a philosophical impossibility. We simply cannot know anything whatever about such things.

. . . .

Jung's description of childhood and old age as periods "without any conscious problems" is of course overstated, but his image of our lives as beginning and ending in submersion in the unconscious explains the different tasks of the hero in the first and second halves of life. At the beginning of life, it takes a hero's effort to mount a consciousness; at the end of life, the hero must be sacrificed in order to accept the unconscious as the final arbiter of the individual's fate.

---

795   In conclusion I would like to come back for a moment to the comparison with the sun. The one hundred and eighty degrees of the arc of life are divisible into four parts. The first quarter, lying to the east, is childhood, that state in which we are a problem for others but are not yet conscious of any problems of our own. Conscious problems fill out the second and third quarters; while in the last, in extreme old age, we descend again into that condition where, regardless of our state of consciousness, we once more become something of a problem for others. Childhood and extreme old age are, of course, utterly different, and yet they have one thing in common: submersion in unconscious psychic happenings. Since the mind of a child grows out of the unconscious its psychic processes, though not easily accessible, are not as difficult to discern as those of a very old person who is sinking again into the unconscious, and who progressively vanishes within it. Childhood and old age are the stages of life without any conscious problems, for which reason I have not taken them into consideration here.

ON THE PSYCHOLOGY OF THE UNCONSCIOUS

Jung realized that the initiation of young men with mother complexes does not mean separation from everything maternal in favor of everything masculine. Often a deepened connection with positive aspects of the mother archetype could help to heal a damaged masculine spirit. Here (in terms somewhat marred by the medical thinking of his time that equated homosexuality with arrested development) Jung describes a young man whose dreams urged this feminine initiatory route in favor of sexual relations with a fraternity brother.

---

67   First I must acquaint the reader in some measure with the personality of the dreamer, for without this acquaintance he will hardly be able to transport himself into the peculiar atmosphere of the dreams. There are dreams that are pure poems and can therefore only be understood through the mood they convey as a whole. The dreamer is a youth of a little over twenty, still entirely boyish in appearance. There is even a touch of girlishness in his looks and manner of expression. The latter betrays a very good education and upbringing. He is intelligent, with pronounced intellectual and aesthetic interests. His aestheticism is very much in evidence: we are made instantly aware of his good taste and his fine appreciation of all forms of art. His feelings are tender and soft, given to the enthusiasms typical of puberty, but somewhat effeminate. There is no trace of adolescent callowness. Undoubtedly he is too young for his age, a clear case of retarded development. It is quite in keeping with this that he should have come to me on account of his homosexuality. The

night preceding his first visit he had the following dream: "*I am in a lofty cathedral filled with mysterious twilight. They tell me that it is the cathedral at Lourdes. In the centre there is a deep dark well, into which I have to descend.*"

168   The dream is clearly a coherent expression of mood. The dreamer's comments are as follows: "Lourdes is the mystic fount of healing. Naturally I remembered yesterday that I was going to you for treatment and was in search of a cure. There is said to be a well like this at Lourdes. It would be rather unpleasant to go down into this water. The well in the church was ever so deep."

169   Now what does dream tell us? On the surface it seems clear enough, and we might be content to take it as a kind of poetic formulation of the mood of the day before. But we should never stop there, for experience shows that dreams are much deeper and more significant. One might almost suppose that the dreamer came to the doctor in a highly poetic mood and was entering upon the treatment as though it were a sacred religious act to be performed in the mystical half-light of some awe-inspiring sanctuary. But this does not fit the facts at all. The patient merely came to the doctor to be treated for that unpleasant matter, his homosexuality, which is anything but poetic. At any rate we cannot see from the mood of the preceding day why he should dream so poetically, if we were to accept so direct a causation for the origin of the dream. But we might conjecture, perhaps, that the dream was stimulated precisely by the dreamer's impressions of that highly unpoetical affair which impelled him to come to me for treatment. We might even suppose that he dreamed in such an intensely poetical manner just because of the unpoeticalness of his mood on the day before, much as a man who has fasted by day dreams of delicious meals at night. It cannot be denied that the thought of treatment, of the cure and its unpleasant procedure, recurs in the dream, but poetically transfigured, in a guise which meets most effectively the lively aesthetic and emotional needs of the dreamer. He will be drawn on irresistibly by this inviting picture, despite the fact that the well is dark, deep, and cold. Something of the dream-mood will persist after sleep and will even linger on into the morning of the day on which he has to submit to the unpleasant and unpoetical duty of visiting me. Perhaps the drab reality will be

touched by the bright, golden after-glow of the dream feeling.

170   Is this, perhaps, the purpose of the dream? That would not be impossible, for in my experience the vast majority of dreams are compensatory.[11] They always stress the other side in order to maintain the psychic equilibrium. But the compensation of mood is not the only purpose of the dream picture. The dream also provides a *mental corrective*. The patient had of course nothing like an adequate understanding of the treatment to which he was about to submit himself. But the dream gives him a picture which describes in poetic metaphors the nature of the treatment before him. This becomes immediately apparent if we follow up his associations and comments on the image of the cathedral: "Cathedral," he says, "makes me think of Cologne Cathedral. Even as a child I was fascinated by it. I remember my mother telling me of it for the first time, and I also remember how, whenever I saw a village church, I used to ask if that were Cologne Cathedral. I wanted to be a priest in a cathedral like that."

171   In these associations the patient is describing a very important experience of his childhood. As in nearly all cases of this kind, he had a particularly close tie with his mother. By this we are not to understand a particularly good or intense *conscious* relationship, but something in the nature of a secret, subterranean tie which expresses itself consciously, perhaps, only in the retarded development of character, i.e., in a relative infantilism. The developing personality naturally veers away from such an unconscious infantile bond; for nothing is more obstructive to development than persistence in an unconscious—we could also say, a psychically embryonic—state. For this reason instinct seizes on the first opportunity to replace the mother by another object. If it is to be a real mother-substitute, this object must be, in some sense, an analogy of her. This is entirely the case with our patient. The intensity with which his childish fantasy seized upon the symbol of Cologne Cathedral corresponds to the strength of his unconscious need to find a substitute for the mother. The unconscious need is heightened still further in a case where the infantile bond could become harmful. Hence the enthusiasm with which his childish imagination took up the idea

11 The idea of compensation has already been extensively used by Alfred Adler.

of the Church; for the Church is, in the fullest sense, a mother. We speak not only of Mother Church, but even of the Church's womb. In the ceremony known as the *benedictio fontis*, the baptismal font is apostrophized as "immaculatus divini fontis uterus"—the immaculate womb of the divine font. We naturally think that a man must have known this meaning consciously before it could get to work in his fantasy, and that an unknowing child could not possibly be affected by these significations. Such analogies certainly do not work by way of the conscious mind, but in quite another manner.

172   The Church represents a higher spiritual substitute for the purely natural, or "carnal," tie to the parents. Consequently it frees the individual from an unconscious natural relationship which, strictly speaking, is not a relationship at all but simply a condition of inchoate, unconscious identity. This, just because it is unconscious, possesses a tremendous inertia and offers the utmost resistance to any kind of spiritual development. It would be hard to say what the essential difference is between this state and the soul of an animal. Now, it is by no means the special prerogative of the Christian Church to try to make it possible for the individual to detach himself from his original, animal-like condition; the Church is simply the latest, and specifically Western, form of an instinctive striving that is probably as old as mankind itself. It is a striving that can be found in the most varied forms among all primitive peoples who are in any way developed and have not yet become degenerate: I mean the institution or rite of initiation into manhood. When he has reached puberty the young man is conducted to the "men's house," or some other place of consecration, where he is systematically alienated from his family. At the same time he is initiated into the religious mysteries, and in this way is ushered not only into a wholly new set of relationships, but, as a renewed and changed personality, into a new world, like one reborn (*quasimodo genitus*). The initiation is often attended by all kinds of tortures, sometimes including such things as circumcision and the like. These practices are undoubtedly very old. They have almost become instinctive mechanisms, with the result that they continue to repeat themselves without external compulsion, as in the "baptisms" of German students or the

even more wildly extravagant initiations in American students' fraternities. They are engraved on the unconscious as a primordial image.

173   When his mother told him as a little boy about Cologne Cathedral, this primordial image was stirred and awakened to life. But there was no priestly instructor to develop it further, so the child remained in his mother's hands. Yet the longing for a man's leadership continued to grow in the boy, taking the form of homosexual leanings—a faulty development that might never have come about had a man been there to educate his childish fantasies. The deviation towards homosexuality has, to be sure, numerous historical precedents. In ancient Greece, as also in certain primitive communities, homosexuality and education were practically synonymous. Viewed in this light, the homosexuality of adolescence is only a misunderstanding of the otherwise very appropriate need for masculine guidance. One might also say that the fear of incest which is based on the mother-complex extends to women in general; but in my opinion an immature man is quite right to be afraid of women, because his relations with women are generally disastrous.

174   According to the dream, then, what the initiation of the treatment signifies for the patient is the fulfilment of the true meaning of his homosexuality, i.e., his entry into the world of the adult man. All that we have been forced to discuss here in such tedious and long-winded detail, in order to understand it properly, the dream has condensed into a few vivid metaphors, thus creating a picture which works far more effectively on the imagination, feeling, and understanding of the dreamer than any learned discourse. Consequently the patient was better and more intelligently prepared for the treatment than if he had been overwhelmed with medical and pedagogical maxims. (For this reason I regard dreams not only as a valuable source of information but as an extraordinarily effective instrument of education.)

175   We come now to the second dream. I must explain in advance that in the first consultation I did not refer in any way to the dream we have just been discussing. It was not even mentioned. Nor was there a word said that was even remotely connected with the foregoing. This is the second dream: *"I am in a great Gothic cathedral. At the altar stands a priest. I stand be-*

fore him with my friend, holding in my hand a little Japanese ivory figure, with the feeling that it is going to be baptized. Suddenly an elderly woman appears, takes the fraternity ring from my friend's finger, and puts it on her own. My friend is afraid that this may bind him in some way. But at the same moment there is a sound of wonderful organ music."

176 Here I will only bring out briefly those points which continue and supplement the dream of the preceding day. The second dream is unmistakably connected with the first: once more the dreamer is in church, that is, in the state of initiation into manhood. But a new figure has been added: the priest, whose absence in the previous situation we have already noted. The dream therefore confirms that the unconscious meaning of his homosexuality has been fulfilled and that a further development can be started. The actual initiation ceremony, namely the baptism, may now begin. The dream symbolism corroborates what I said before, namely that it is not the prerogative of the Christian Church to bring about such transitions and psychic transformations, but that behind the Church there is a living primordial image which in certain conditions is capable of enforcing them.

177 What, according to the dream, is to be baptized is a little Japanese ivory figure. The patient says of this: "It was a tiny, grotesque little manikin that reminded me of the male organ. It was certainly odd that this member was to be baptized. But after all, with the Jews circumcision is a sort of baptism. That must be a reference to my homosexuality, because the friend standing with me before the altar is the one with whom I have sexual relations. We belong to the same fraternity. The fraternity ring obviously stands for our relationship."

178 We know that in common usage the ring is the token of a bond or relationship, as for example the wedding ring. We can therefore safely take the fraternity ring in this case as symbolizing the homosexual relationship, and the fact that the dreamer appears together with his friend points in the same direction.

179 The complaint to be remedied is homosexuality. The dreamer is to be led out of this relatively childish condition and initiated into the adult state by means of a kind of circumcision ceremony under the supervision of a priest. These ideas correspond exactly to my analysis of the previous dream. Thus far the development has proceeded logically and consistently with the

aid of archetypal images. But now a disturbing factor comes on the scene. An elderly woman suddenly takes possession of the fraternity ring; in other words, she draws to herself what has hitherto been a homosexual relationship, thus causing the dreamer to fear that he is getting involved in a new relationship with obligations of its own. Since the ring is now on the hand of a woman, a marriage of sorts has been contracted, i.e., the homosexual relationship seems to have passed over into a heterosexual one, but a heterosexual relationship of a peculiar kind since it concerns an elderly woman. "She is a friend of my mother's," says the patient. "I am very fond of her, in fact she is like a mother to me."

180   From this remark we can see what has happened in the dream: as a result of the initiation the homosexual tie has been cut and a heterosexual relationship substituted for it, a platonic friendship with a motherly type of woman. In spite of her resemblance to his mother, this woman is not his mother any longer, so the relationship with her signifies a step beyond the mother towards masculinity, and hence a partial conquest of his adolescent homosexuality.

181   The fear of the new tie can easily be understood, firstly as fear which the woman's resemblance to his mother might naturally arouse—it might be that the dissolution of the homosexual tie has led to a complete regression to the mother—and secondly as fear of the new and unknown factors in the adult heterosexual state with its possible obligations, such as marriage, etc. That we are in fact concerned here not with a regression but with a progression seems to be confirmed by the music that now peals forth. The patient is musical and especially susceptible to solemn organ music. Therefore music signifies for him a very positive feeling, so in this case it forms a harmonious conclusion to the dream, which in its turn is well qualified to leave behind a beautiful, holy feeling for the following morning.

182   If you consider the fact that up to now the patient had seen me for only one consultation, in which little more was discussed than a general anamnesis, you will doubtless agree with me when I say that both dreams make astonishing anticipations. They show the patient's situation in a highly remarkable light, and one that is very strange to the conscious mind, while at the same time lending to the banal medical situation an aspect that

is uniquely attuned to the mental peculiarities of the dreamer, and thus capable of stringing his aesthetic, intellectual, and religious interests to concert pitch. No better conditions for treatment could possibly be imagined. One is almost persuaded, from the meaning of these dreams, that the patient entered upon the treatment with the utmost readiness and hopefulness, quite prepared to cast aside his boyishness and become a man. In reality, however, this was not the case at all. Consciously he was full of hesitation and resistance; moreover, as the treatment progressed, he constantly showed himself antagonistic and difficult, ever ready to slip back into his previous infantilism. Consequently the dreams stand in strict contrast to his conscious behaviour. They move along a progressive line and take the part of the educator. They clearly reveal their special function. This function I have called compensation. The unconscious progressiveness and the conscious regressiveness together form a pair of opposites which, as it were, keeps the scales balanced. The influence of the educator tilts the balance in favour of progression.

183   In the case of this young man the images of the collective unconscious play an entirely positive role, which comes from the fact that he has no really dangerous tendency to fall back on a fantasy-substitute for reality and to entrench himself behind it against life. The effect of these unconscious images has something fateful about it. Perhaps—who knows?—these eternal images are what men mean by fate.

LECTURE VIII, 13 March 1929

In the following transcription from his 1929 English Seminar on dreams, Jung discusses the masculine archetype of the *puer aeternus*, the eternal boy who is so often a personification of the immature eros of a man. Jung saw the immaturity of eros as characteristic of the masculine nature. The inner recognition of this problem, as in the dream that is discussed here, was the first step to its solution.

Next dream [12], *the same night:* There is an extraordinary difference between the next dream and the last, with a most remarkable compensation. "I am in a bedroom with my wife, and I see a door which leads into another room slowly open. I immediately go to the door, push it open, and in the other room I find a little boy completely naked. I carry him into the bedroom and I am convinced in the dream that he is not a natural boy. In order to prevent his getting away (he is struggling in my arms) I press him against me, and he gives me the most remarkable feeling (not at all a sexual feeling) of satisfaction as if this true thing were satisfactory to the longings of my feelings. Then my wife brings in a variety of food for the child. I see black bread and white bread. The child does not want to eat the black bread but eats the white. Then suddenly he flies out of the window and beckons to us from the air."

Associations: Door slowly opening: An allusion to a passage in the second part of *Faust* when Faust is getting old and has been trying to live a rational life. There is a monologue about the fact that he likes to think along the rational lines of the day and be scientific; then night comes and all is different, the door opens and no one

45

comes in! We cannot do without magic. In the man's dream the door opens and no one comes in.[6] That means something supernatural. He has studied occultism, and he uses the word exteriorization, the theory of what formerly was attributed to spirits, table-tipping, rapping, noises in the wall. His theory is that it is not done by a ghost but by something in ourselves, the exteriorizing of psychological contents, and the dreamer is convinced of the reality of such facts. In the dream he has the feeling that the door is opening in a queer way. So he goes to see and finds the little naked boy in the other room.

The boy: The only association he had is the traditional representation of Eros, the naked baby boy. It gives a peculiar satisfaction to his feelings when he presses the boy against him.

Bread: The black bread is more nourishing than the white because it contains a protein in the silver skin of the grain. "The little amourette has not been fed in the right way by my wife, therefore he flies away and is beckoning from afar." Here you get a precious piece of masculine psychology. I am giving the whole sex away! That dream needs some mending. It is a good dream, an intimate, personal dream. How do you explain it after such an objective dream?

Dr. Binger: The contents are much the same. He sees himself as a child, Eros his infantile self. In the other dream he projected himself into his father, so he himself was a child.

Dr. Jung: Well, that needs discussion. I think we had better begin with the text to be sure that we are going right. The dreamer is in the bedroom with his wife, therefore it means in an intimate situation with his wife. That statement in the dream before, that he has to deal with his highest values and not with his lowest, leads

---

[6] *Faust,* Part II, Act V, in the tr. of Louis MacNeice (*Goethe's Faust,* London, 1951), p. 281:

> "But now such spectredom so throngs the air
> That none knows how to dodge it, none knows where.
> Though one day greet us with a rational gleam,
> The night entangles us in webs of dream.
> We come back happy from the fields of spring—
> And a bird croaks. Croaks what? Some evil thing.
> Enmeshed in superstition night and morn,
> It forms and shows itself and comes to warn.
> And we, so scared, stand without friend or kin,
> And the door creaks—and nobody comes in."

him to his intimate problem with his wife. Something in the business does not work, something in his relation to his wife does not work. The man who leads a provisional life does not deal with Eros. His father knows all about that, so he does not have to bother about it. He can close his eyes to the whole Eros side, and he is not adapted to his wife at all. You cannot deal with a woman with mere objectivity, so it is quite natural that in this dream the obstacle appears. The dream leads him right into the bedroom, for it is also a sexual trouble, sex being the strongest and clearest expression of relatedness. In this situation, certain contents of the unconscious seem to be exteriorized. As far as my knowledge reaches, those contents of the unconscious that are so near, so close that they are almost conscious, have a tendency to get exteriorized. They are almost ready to burst into consciousness, but certain obstacles are in the way and they are exteriorized. Here we have a little miracle. I have no prejudice against these little miracles. Such peculiar things take place occasionally, but how they are connected with our psychology God knows, I don't. Only fools think that everything can be explained. The true substance of the world is inexplicable. In this case it should dawn upon the dreamer that the thing lacking in his relation to his wife is Eros. It is almost a miracle that he has not seen it. It is Eros that ought to come in. He opens the door but no one comes in, then he finds the little boy in the other room and he holds him in his arms for a minute, feeling a peculiar satisfaction when he presses the child against him, and he thinks it is odd that it is not a sexual feeling. That is one of the foolish ideas which men have. They think that Eros is sex, but not at all, Eros is relatedness. Woman has something to say to that! He likes to think that it is a sexual problem, but it is not, it is an Eros problem.

Bread: Black bread would be more nourishing, yet the child refuses it and eats the white bread.

Dr. Shaw: Does the black bread stand for his thinking, his superior function?

Dr. Jung: There is no sign of that.

Miss Bianchi: He stresses the difference between the white and the black, the contrast. Can one assume that it has something to do with the nature of the two people?

Dr. Jung: I am not so sure of that. I would say that bread suggests food. Our mind, heart, body, every function must have its specific food, to continue living, so Eros cannot live without being fed. The food given to Eros is here called bread. Black and white is the ordinary symbolism for moral values. White is innocence, purity; black is earth dirt, night, Hell. The very black bread (pumpernickel) is very heavy and not easy to digest. They have a very primitive way of grinding the grain, so that all the husks are left in. It makes moist and heavy bread, but it is very nourishing. The boy refuses the black bread and accepts the white. What does that mean?

Mr. Gibb: He accepts the more idealistic.

Dr. Jung: The dreamer is much concerned with the kind of food he eats himself. He has a complex about food, and if you study such complexes you always find something interesting behind them. White bread is made from the very heart of the grain and the husks are thrown away, or given to the swine, so white bread gives the idea of luxury, nobility, or soul. It is made from the "soul" of the grain. The people who eat only white bread are noble, fine people, and those who eat black bread are coarse, vulgar, plebeian, earthy. Now, the question is whether the child is fed with heavy substantial food of the earth. To our Christian conscience that means food of devils and Hell. What is of the earth, earthy? Sexuality! But the general assumption that Eros is fed on sexuality is wrong. Curiously enough, he is fed only on white bread, on the very heart of the grain, by something hidden within sexuality, that is the *feeling*, the *relatedness*. If I should say to the patient, "Having sexual intercourse with your wife does not prove that you are related to her," he would not understand, for he thinks it would. You have relatedness by your feeling, by your rapport, and that is what feeds Eros. One expects that after sexual intercourse the soul should not be sad, but often the worst fights and misunderstandings in marriage happen after sexual intercourse, because sexuality does not feed Eros. This is often the direct cause of quarrels and separations.

The dream so far is a very important realization. Eros comes in a miraculous way and disappears in a miraculous way. He flies out of the window. What does that mean?

Dr. Binger: The man is not ready for a feeling relation.

Dr. Jung: We don't know what Eros would do if he stayed long enough. He might feed on the black bread too after a while, but he does not stay long enough. He just says, "Nothing doing; goodbye!" It is a good joke and a terrible truth. It is the promised land, but only for a moment is the fleeting vision clear; then he flies away before he can feed on the black bread. This is often the way in analysis. Just for a moment you see the way ahead quite clearly, then the vision vanishes, the mist gathers, and again you are in confusion. It is a sudden vision of the truth that appears and vanishes again without concretization. Eating the bread in his house is an archaic symbol for hospitality. But Eros does not eat all the bread, only the white, then he disappears, beckoning from afar, "Au revoir, nice to have seen you, perhaps I will see you again, it's not quite certain."

Mrs. Sigg: I have some doubt about the boy being only Eros. In *Faust*, the boy had something to do with poetry and imagination. He was something else.

Dr. Jung: True, he may not be Eros alone. I have my doubts too. But I kept to Eros as the dreamer was unaware of the general quality of his dream. One could say that the fact that he associated with Faust in the beginning points to the charioteer, Homunculus, and Euphorion,[7] the three forms of that element which I technically term the Puer Aeternus symbol in dreams. To my mind it refers to this symbolism. After the father complex, the infantile complex necessarily appears, where he is the son. First he turned his eyes to the father, now he is the son, still in the psychology of a boy of eight or ten years, so the Eros figure would be the infantile side of the dreamer. But if you say that, then the infantile side is to come into relation with his wife, and he isn't quite up to that situation yet. You could say that his natural unsophisticated feeling had better come into relation with his wife. It is quite true that the child is the infantile side of the dreamer, but it is also the promising thing in him. The things which one has developed are finished, but the undeveloped things are still a promise for the future. So the boy represents what may be developed, the self-renewing thing in man, and a good term to give to this figure is the Puer Aeternus. The old idea was that the Puer Aeternus was a Divine Child who eternally appeared and disappeared in a miraculous way. The Etruscan boy Tages,[8] a little naked boy, appears in the furrow

[7] *Faust*, Part II, Act II. A summary of the fates of these three figures is given at the beginning of the lecture of 27 March 1929, below.

[8] For Tages, the legendary founder of Etruscan augural lore, and Oannes, mentioned a few lines further, see CW 5, pars. 291-2. Adonis was a Phoenician vegetation god and Tammuz his Babylonian equivalent.

where the peasant is ploughing, and he teaches the people laws, arts, and culture. Adonis was such a boy. Tammuz appears to the women every spring. The Babylonian fish-god Oannes comes out of the water as a fish, appears at sunrise, and teaches the people agriculture, laws, etc., during the day, disappearing at night into the sea again. Meister Eckhart had a vision of a little naked boy who visited him.[9] Then there are some English fairy stories of the radiant boy, in which the vision of the boy is always unlucky, sometimes absolutely fatal. There must be some reason for this, I do not know what it may be. The Puer Aeternus[10] is simply the personification of the infantile side of our character, repressed because it is infantile. If the dreamer allows that element to come in, it is as though he himself had disappeared and come back as a little naked boy. Then if his wife could accept him as such, everything would be all right. The little boy ought to be brought up, educated, perhaps spanked. If the inferior element can enter life, then there is a promise of future life, things can develop, there can be progress. In mythology, the figure of this little naked boy has an almost divine creative character. As the Puer Aeternus he appears in a miraculous way and then disappears in the same way. In *Faust* he has three forms: Boy Charioteer, Homunculus, Euphorion. They were all destroyed by fire, which meant in Goethe's case that the Pueri Aeterni all disappeared in a passionate outbreak. Fire puts an end to everything, even an end to the world. Fire that is the sap of culture can burst forth and destroy everything. This happens from time to time, as for instance in the Bolshevist Revolution, when the cultural form could not hold the tension of energy any more, and the fire broke forth and destroyed the Russian civilization.

[9] For further details see below, p. 188.
[10] Jung was to develop this theme later in "The Psychology of the Child Archetype" (1941), CW 9 i.

THE LOVE PROBLEM OF A STUDENT

Jung saw the early love-relationships, whether homosexual or heterosexual, as places where eros could be cultivated.

---

216   As to whether student marriages are premature, we must take note of a fact that applies to all early marriages, namely, that a girl of twenty is usually older than a man of twenty-five, as far as maturity of judgment is concerned. With many men of twenty-five the period of psychological puberty is not yet over. Puberty is a period of illusion and only partial responsibility. The psychological difference is due to the fact that a boy, up to the time of sexual maturity, is as a rule quite childish, whereas a girl develops much earlier than he does the psychological subtleties that go hand in hand with adolescence. Into this childishness sexuality often breaks with brutal force, while, despite the onset of puberty, it often goes on slumbering in a girl until the passion of love awakens it. There are a surprising number of women whose real sexuality, even though they are married, remains virginal for years; they become conscious of it only when they fall in love with another man. That is the reason why very many women have no understanding at all of masculine sexuality—they are completely unconscious of their own. With men it is different. Sexuality bursts on them like a tempest, filling them with brute desires and needs, and there is scarcely one of them who escapes the painful problem of masturbation. But a girl can masturbate for years without knowing what she is doing.

217   The onrush of sexuality in a boy brings about a powerful

51

change in his psychology. He now has the sexuality of a grown man with the soul of a child. Often the flood of obscene fantasies and smutty talk with schoolfellows pours like a torrent of dirty water over all his delicate and childish feelings, sometimes smothering them for ever. Unexpected moral conflicts arise, temptations of every description lie in wait for him and weave themselves into his fantasies. The psychic assimilation of the sexual complex causes him the greatest difficulties even though he may not be conscious of its existence. The onset of puberty also brings about considerable changes in his metabolism, as can be seen from the pimples and acne that so often afflict adolescents. The psyche is disturbed in a similar manner and thrown off its balance. At this age the young man is full of illusions, which are always a sign of psychic disequilibrium. They make stability and maturity of judgment impossible. His tastes, his interests, his plans alter fitfully. He can suddenly fall head over heels in love with a girl, and a fortnight later he cannot conceive how anything of the sort could have happened to him. He is so riddled with illusions that he actually needs these mistakes to make him conscious of his own taste and individual judgment. He is still experimenting with life, and *must* experiment with it in order to learn how to judge things correctly. Hence there are very few men who have not had sexual experience of some kind before they are married. During puberty it is mostly homosexual experiences, and these are much more common than is generally admitted. Heterosexual experiences come later, not always of a very beautiful kind. For the less the sexual complex is assimilated to the whole of the personality, the more autonomous and instinctive it will be. Sexuality is then purely animal and recognizes no psychological distinctions. The most inferior woman will do; it is enough if she has the typical secondary sexual characteristics. A false step of this kind does not entitle us to draw conclusions about a man's character, as the act can easily occur at a time when the sexual complex is still split off from the psyche's influence. Nevertheless, too many experiences of this nature have a bad effect on the formation of the personality, as by force of habit they fix sexuality on too low a level and make it unacceptable to moral judgment. The result is that though the man in question is outwardly a respectable citizen, inwardly he is prey to sexual fantasies of the lowest kind, or else he represses them and on some festive occasion they come leaping to the surface in their primitive form, much to the astonishment of his unsuspecting wife—assuming, of course, that she notices what is going on. A frequent accompaniment is premature coldness towards the wife. Women are often frigid from the first day of marriage because their sensation function does not respond to this kind of sexuality in their husbands. The weakness of a man's judgment at the time of psychological puberty should prompt him to reflect very deeply on the premature choice of a wife.

218   Let us now turn to other forms of relationship between the sexes that are customary during the student period. There are, as you know, characteristic liaisons between students, chiefly in the great universities of other countries. These relationships are sometimes fairly stable and may even have a psychological value, as they do not consist entirely of sexuality but also, in part, of love. Occasionally the liaison is continued into marriage. The relationship stands, therefore, considerably higher than prostitution. But as a rule it is limited to those students who were careful in the choice of their parents. It is usually a question of money, for most of the girls are dependent on their lovers for financial help, though they could not be said to sell their love for money. Very often the relationship is a beautiful episode in the girl's life, otherwise poor and empty, while for the man it may be his first intimate acquaintance with a woman, and in later life a memory on which he looks back with emotion. Often, again, there is nothing valuable in these affairs, partly owing to the man's crude sensuality, thoughtlessness, and lack of feeling, and partly owing to the frivolity and fickleness of the girl.

219   Over all these relationships hangs the Damoclean sword of their transitoriness, which prevents the formation of real values. They are passing episodes, experiments of very limited validity. Their injurious effect on the personality is due to the fact that the man gets the girl too easily, so that the value of the love-object is depreciated. It is convenient for him to dispose of his sexual problem in such a simple and irresponsible way. He becomes spoilt. But even more, the fact that he is sexually satisfied robs him of a driving-force which no young man can do without. He becomes blasé and can afford to wait. Meanwhile he

can calmly review the massed femininity passing before him until the right party turns up. Then the wedding comes along and the latest date is thrown over. This procedure adds little of advantage to his character. The low level of relationship tends to keep sexuality on a correspondingly low level of development, and this can easily lead to difficulties in marriage. Or if his sexual fantasies are repressed, the result is only too likely to be a neurotic or, worse still, a moral zealot.

220   Homosexual relations between students of either sex are by no means uncommon. So far as I can judge of this phenomenon, I would say that these relationships are less common with us, and on the continent generally, than in certain other countries where boy and girl college students live in strict segregation. I am speaking here not of pathological homosexuals who are incapable of real friendship and meet with little sympathy among normal individuals, but of more or less normal youngsters who enjoy such a rapturous friendship that they also express their feelings in sexual form. With them it is not just a matter of mutual masturbation, which in all school and college life is the order of the day among the younger age groups, but of a higher and more spiritual form which deserves the name "friendship" in the classical sense of the word. When such a friendship exists between an older man and a younger its educative significance is undeniable. A slightly homosexual teacher, for example, often owes his brilliant educational gifts to his homosexual disposition. The homosexual relation between an older and a younger man can thus be of advantage to both sides and have a lasting value. An indispensable condition for the value of such a relation is the steadfastness of the friendship and their loyalty to it. But only too often this condition is lacking. The more homosexual a man is, the more prone he is to disloyalty and to the seduction of boys. Even when loyalty and true friendship prevail the results may be undesirable for the development of personality. A friendship of this kind naturally involves a special cult of feeling, of the feminine element in a man. He becomes gushing, soulful, aesthetic, over-sensitive, etc. —in a word, effeminate, and this womanish behaviour is detrimental to his character.

221   Similar advantages and disadvantages can be pointed out in friendships between women, only here the difference in age

54

and the educative factor are not so important. The main value lies in the exchange of tender feelings on the one hand and of intimate thoughts on the other. Generally they are high-spirited, intellectual, and rather masculine women who are seeking to maintain their superiority and to defend themselves against men. Their attitude to men is therefore one of disconcerting self-assurance, with a trace of defiance. Its effect on their character is to reinforce their masculine traits and to destroy their feminine charm. Often a man discovers their homosexuality only when he notices that these women leave him stone-cold.

222   Normally, the practice of homosexuality is not prejudicial to later heterosexual activity. Indeed, the two can even exist side by side. I know a very intelligent woman who spent her whole life as a homosexual and then at fifty entered into a normal relationship with a man.

223   Among the sexual relations of the student period we must mention yet another, which is quite normal even if rather peculiar. This is the attachment of a young man to an older woman, possibly married or at any rate widowed. You will perhaps remember Jean Jacques Rousseau and his connection with Mme de Warens; this is the kind of relationship I have in mind. The man is usually rather shy, unsure of himself, inwardly afraid, sometimes infantile. He naturally seeks a mother, perhaps because he has had too much or too little love in his own family. Many women like nothing better than a man who is rather helpless, especially when they are considerably older than he is; they do not love a man's strength, his virtues and his merits, but his weaknesses. They find his infantilisms charming. If he stammers a little, he is enchanting; or perhaps he has a limp, and this excites maternal compassion and a little more besides. As a rule the woman seduces him, and he willingly submits to her mothering.

224   Not always, however, does a timid youth remain half a child. It may be that this surfeit of maternal solicitude was just what was needed to bring his undeveloped masculinity to the surface. In this way the woman educates his feeling and brings it to full consciousness. He learns to understand a woman who has experience of life and the world, is sure of herself, and thus he has a rare opportunity for a glimpse behind the scenes. But he

can take advantage of it only if he quickly outgrows this relationship, for should he get stuck in it her mothering would ruin him. Maternal tenderness is the most pernicious poison for anyone who has to equip himself for the hard and pitiless struggle of life. If he cannot let go of her apron-strings he will become a spineless parasite—for most of these women have money—and sink to the level of a lap-dog or a pet cat.

225 We must now discuss those forms of relationship which offer no solution of the sexual question for the reason that they are asexual or "platonic." If there were any reliable statistics on this subject, I believe they would show that in Switzerland the majority of students prefer a platonic relationship. Naturally, this raises the question of sexual abstinence. One often hears that abstaining from sexual intercouse is injurious to health. This view is incorrect, at least for people of the student age. Abstinence is injurious to health only when a man has reached the age when he could win a woman for himself, and should do so according to his individual inclinations. The extraordinary intensification of the sexual need that is so often felt at this time has the biological aim of forcibly eliminating the man's scruples, misgivings, doubts, and hesitations. This is very necessary, because the very idea of marriage, with all its doubtful possibilities, often makes a man panicky. It is only to be expected, therefore, that nature will push him over the obstacle. Abstention from sexual intercourse may certainly have injurious effects under these conditions, but not when there is no urgent physical or psychological need for it.

226 This brings us to the very similar question concerning the injurious effects of masturbation. When for physical or psychological reasons normal intercouse is impossible, masturbation as a safety-valve has no ill effects. Young people who come to the doctor suffering from the harmful effects of masturbation are not by any means excessive masturbationists—these usually have no need of a doctor because they are not in any sense ill —rather, their masturbation has harmful effects because it shows psychic complications and is attended by pangs of conscience or by a riot of sexual fantasies. The latter are particularly common among women. Masturbation with psychic complications is harmful, but not the ordinary, uncomplicated kind. If, however, it is continued up to the age when normal intercourse

becomes physically, psychologically, and socially possible, and is indulged in merely in order to avoid the necessary tasks of life, then it is harmful.

227   Platonic relationships are very important during the student period. The form they most commonly take is flirting. Flirting is the expression of an experimental attitude which is altogether appropriate at this age. It is a voluntary activity which, by tacit agreement, puts neither side under an obligation. This is an advantage and at the same time a disadvantage. The experimental attitude enables both parties to get to know each other without any immediately undesirable results. Both exercise their judgment and their skill in self-expression, adaptation, and defence. An enormous variety of experiences which are uncommonly valuable in later life can be picked up from flirting. On the other hand, the absence of any obligation can easily lead to one's becoming an habitual flirt, shallow, frivolous, and heartless. The man turns into a drawing-room hero and professional heart-breaker, never dreaming what a boring figure he cuts; the girl a coquette, and a serious man instinctively feels that she is not to be taken seriously.

228   A phenomenon that is as rare as flirting is common is the conscious cultivation of a serious love. We might call this simply the ideal, without, however, identifying it with traditional romanticism. For the development of personality, there can be no doubt that the timely awakening and conscious cultivation of deeply serious and responsible feelings are of the utmost value. A relationship of this kind can be the most effective shield against the temptations that beset a young man, as well as being a powerful incentive to hard work, loyalty, and reliability. However, there is no value so great that it does not have its unfavourable side. A relationship that is too ideal easily becomes exclusive. Through his love the young man is too much cut off from the acquaintance of other women, and the girl does not learn the art of erotic conquest because she has got her man already. Woman's instinct for possession is a dangerous thing, and it may easily happen that the man will regret all the experiences he never had with women before marriage and will make up for them afterwards.

229   Hence it must not be concluded that every relationship of this kind is ideal. There are cases where the exact opposite is

true—when, for instance, a man or girl trails round with a school sweetheart for no intelligible reason, from mere force of habit. Whether from inertia, or lack of spirit, or helplessness they simply cannot get rid of each other. Perhaps the parents on both sides find the match suitable, and the affair, begun in a moment of thoughtlessness and prolonged by habit, is passively accepted as a *fait accompli.* Here the disadvantages pile up without a single advantage. For the development of personality, acquiescence and passivity are harmful because they are an obstacle to valuable experience and to the exercise of one's specific gifts and virtues. Moral qualities are won only in freedom and prove their worth only in morally dangerous situations. The thief who refrains from stealing merely because he is in prison is not a moral personality. Though the parents may gaze benignly on this touching marriage and add their children's respectability to the tale of their own virtues, it is all a sham and a delusion, lacking real strength, and sapped by moral inertia.

230   After this brief survey of the problems as we meet them in actual life, I will, in conclusion, turn to the land of heart's desire and utopian possibilities.

231   Nowadays we can hardly discuss the love problem without speaking of the utopia of free love, including trial marriage. I regard this idea as a wishful fantasy and an attempt to make light of a problem which in actual life is invariably very difficult. It is no more possible to make life easy than it is to grow a herb of immortality. The force of gravity can be overcome only by the requisite application of energy. Similarly, the solution of the love problem challenges all our resources. Anything else would be useless patchwork. Free love would be conceivable only if everyone were capable of the highest moral achievement. The idea of free love was not invented with this aim in view, but merely to make something difficult appear easy. Love requires depth and loyalty of feeling; without them it is not love but mere caprice. True love will always commit itself and engage in lasting ties; it needs freedom only to effect its choice, not for its accomplishment. Every true and deep love is a sacrifice. The lover sacrifices all other possibilities, or rather, the illusion that such possibilities exist. If this sacrifice is not made, his illusions prevent the growth of any deep and responsible

feeling, so that the very possibility of experiencing real love is denied him.

232   Love has more than one thing in common with religious faith. It demands unconditional trust and expects absolute surrender. Just as nobody but the believer who surrenders himself wholly to God can partake of divine grace, so love reveals its highest mysteries and its wonder only to those who are capable of unqualified devotion and loyalty of feeling. And because this is so difficult, few mortals can boast of such an achievement. But, precisely because the truest and most devoted love is also the most beautiful, let no man seek to make it easy. He is a sorry knight who shrinks from the difficulty of loving his lady. Love is like God: both give themselves only to their bravest knights.

233   I would offer the same criticism of trial marriages. The very fact that a man enters into a marriage on trial means that he is making a reservation; he wants to be sure of not burning his fingers, to risk nothing. But that is the most effective way of forestalling any real experience. You do not experience the terrors of the Polar ice by perusing a travel-book, or climb the Himalayas in a cinema.

234   Love is not cheap—let us therefore beware of cheapening it! All our bad qualities, our egotism, our cowardice, our worldly wisdom, our cupidity—all these would persuade us not to take love seriously. But love will reward us only when we do. I must even regard it as a misfortune that nowadays the sexual question is spoken of as something distinct from love. The two questions should not be separated, for when there is a sexual problem it can be solved only by love. Any other solution would be a harmful substitute. Sexuality dished out as sexuality is brutish; but sexuality as an expression of love is hallowed. Therefore, never ask what a man does, but how he does it. If he does it from love or in the spirit of love, then he serves a god; and whatever he may do is not ours to judge, for it is ennobled.

235   I trust that these remarks will have made it clear to you that I pass no sort of moral judgment on sexuality as a natural phenomenon, but prefer to make its moral evaluation dependent on the way it is expressed.

III. THE FATHER

THE SIGNIFICANCE OF THE FATHER IN THE DESTINY OF THE INDIVIDUAL

Case 2

707 A man of thirty-four, of small build, with a clever, kindly expression. He was easily embarrassed, blushed often. He had come for treatment on account of "nervousness." He said he was very irritable, readily fatigued, had nervous stomach-trouble, was often so deeply depressed that he sometimes thought of suicide.

708 Before coming to me for treatment he had sent me a circumstantial autobiography, or rather a history of his illness, in order to prepare me for his visit. His story began: "My father was a very big and strong man." This sentence awakened my curiosity; I turned over a page and there read: "When I was fifteen a big lad of nineteen took me into a wood and indecently assaulted me."

709 The numerous gaps in the patient's story induced me to obtain a more exact anamnesis from him, which led to the following disclosures: The patient was the youngest of three brothers. His father, a big, red-haired man, was formerly a soldier in the Swiss Guard at the Vatican; later he became a policeman. He was a stern, gruff old soldier, who brought up his sons with military discipline; he issued commands, did not call them by name, but whistled for them. He had spent his youth in Rome, and during his gay life there had contracted syphilis, from the consequences of which he still suffered in old age. He was fond of talking about his adventures in early life. His eldest son (considerably older than the patient) was exactly like him, a big, strong man with red hair. The mother was an ailing woman, prematurely aged. Exhausted and tired of life, she died at forty when the patient was eight years old. He preserved a tender and beautiful memory of his mother.

61

710   At school he was always the whipping-boy and always the object of his schoolfellows' mockery. He thought his peculiar dialect might be to blame. Later he was apprenticed to a strict and unkind master, with whom he stuck it out for over two years, under conditions so trying that all the other apprentices ran away. At fifteen the assault already mentioned took place, together with several other, milder homosexual experiences. Then fate packed him off to France. There he made the acquaintance of a man from the south, a great boaster and Don Juan. He dragged the patient to a brothel; he went unwillingly and out of fear, and found he was impotent. Later he went to Paris, where his eldest brother, a master-mason and the replica of his father, was leading a dissolute life. The patient stayed there a long time, badly paid and helping his sister-in-law out of pity. The brother often took him along to a brothel, but he was always impotent.

711   One day his brother asked him to make over to him his inheritance, 6,000 francs. The patient consulted his second brother, who was also in Paris, and who urgently tried to dissuade him from handing over the money, because it would only be squandered. Nevertheless the patient went and gave his inheritance to his brother, who naturally ran through it in the shortest possible time. And the second brother, who would have dissuaded him, was also let in for 500 francs. To my astonished question why he had so light-heartedly given the money to his brother without any guarantee he replied: well, he asked for it. He was not a bit sorry about the money, he would give him another 6,000 francs if he had it. The eldest brother afterwards went to the bad altogether and his wife divorced him.

712   The patient returned to Switzerland and remained for a year without regular employment, often suffering from hunger. During this time he made the acquaintance of a family and became a frequent visitor. The husband belonged to some peculiar sect, was a hypocrite, and neglected his family. The wife was elderly, ill, and weak, and moreover pregnant. There were six children, all living in great poverty. For this woman the patient developed a warm affection and shared with her the little he possessed. She told him her troubles, saying she felt sure she would die in childbed. He promised her (although he possessed nothing) that he would take charge of the children and bring them up. The

woman did die in childbed, but the orphanage interfered and allowed him only one child. So now he had a child but no family, and naturally could not bring it up by himself. He thus came to think of marrying. But as he had never yet fallen in love with a girl he was in great perplexity.

713   It then occurred to him that his elder brother was divorced from his wife, and he resolved to marry her. He wrote to her in Paris, saying what he intended. She was seventeen years older than he, but not averse to his plan. She invited him to come to Paris to talk matters over. But on the eve of the journey fate willed that he should run an iron nail into his foot, so that he could not travel. After a while, when the wound was healed, he went to Paris and found that he had imagined his sister-in-law, now his fiancée, to be younger and prettier than she really was. The wedding took place, however, and three months later the first coitus, on his wife's initiative. He himself had no desire for it. They brought up the child together, he in the Swiss and she in the Parisian fashion, as she was a French woman. At the age of nine the child was run over and killed by a cyclist. The patient then felt very lonely and dismal at home. He proposed to his wife that they should adopt a young girl, whereupon she broke out into a fury of jealousy. Then, for the first time in his life, he fell in love with a young girl, and simultaneously the neurosis started with deep depression and nervous exhaustion, for meanwhile his life at home had become a hell.

714   My suggestion that he should separate from his wife was dismissed out of hand, on the ground that he could not take it upon himself to make the old woman unhappy on his account. He obviously preferred to go on being tormented, for the memories of his youth seemed to him more precious than any present joys.

715   This patient, too, moved all through his life in the magic circle of the family constellation. The strongest and most fateful factor was the relationship to the father; its masochistic-homosexual colouring is clearly apparent in everything he did. Even the unfortunate marriage was determined by the father, for the patient married the divorced wife of his elder brother, which amounted to marrying his mother. At the same time, his wife was the mother-substitute for the woman who died in childbed. The neurosis set in the moment the libido was withdrawn from

the infantile relationship and for the first time came a bit nearer to an individually determined goal. In this as in the previous case, the family constellation proved to be by far the stronger, so that the narrow field of neurosis was all that was left over for the struggling individuality.

. . . .

Jung revised this early essay forty years after its first publication.* It shows an evolution of his understanding from a time when the father complex seemed to him entirely an effect of the personal father to his mature years when he had come to appreciate the ambivalent archetype to which experiences of a father are assimilated. All archetypes contain positive and negative features, but where the mother archetype tends to split into positive and negative images, the father archetype tends to combine its opposites into a single ambiguous image of seductive and paralyzing power.

Case 4

731   An eight-year-old boy, intelligent, rather delicate-looking, brought to me by his mother on account of enuresis. During the consultation the child clung all the time to his mother, a pretty, youthful woman. The marriage was a happy one, but the father was strict, and the boy (the eldest child) was rather afraid of him. The mother compensated for the father's strictness by a corresponding tenderness, to which the boy responded so much that he never got away from his mother's apron-strings. He never played with his school-fellows, never went alone into the street unless he had to go to school. He feared the boys' roughness and violence and played thoughtful games at home or helped his mother with the housework. He was extremely jealous of his father, and could not bear it when the father showed tenderness to the mother.

* [Ed. Note. Passages added to the 1949 version are given in angle brackets, and passages replaced or omitted from the 1909 version are given in square brackets in the footnotes.]

732   I took the boy aside and asked him about his dreams. Very often he dreamt of a *black snake that wanted to bite his face.* Then he would cry out, and his mother had to come to him from the next room and stay by his bedside.

733   In the evening he would go quietly to bed. But when falling asleep it seemed to him that a *wicked black man with a sword or a gun was lying on his bed, a tall thin man who wanted to kill him.* The parents slept in the next room. The boy often dreamt that something dreadful was going on in there, as if there were *great black snakes or evil men who wanted to kill Mama.* Then he would cry out, and Mama came to comfort him. Every time he wet his bed he called his mother, who would then have to change the bedclothes.

734   The father was a tall thin man. Every morning he stood naked at the wash-stand in full view of the boy, to perform a thorough ablution. The boy also told me that at night he often started up from sleep at the sound of strange noises in the next room; then he was always horribly afraid that something dreadful was going on in there, a struggle of some kind, but his mother would quiet him and say it was nothing.

735   It is not difficult to see what was happening in the next room. It is equally easy to understand the boy's aim in calling out for his mother: he was jealous and was separating her from the father. He did this also in the daytime whenever he saw his father caressing her. Thus far the boy was simply the father's rival for his mother's love.

736   But now comes the fact that the snake and the wicked man threaten him as well: the same thing happens to him as happens to his mother in the next room. To that extent he identifies with his mother and thus puts himself in a similar relationship to the father. This is due to his homosexual component, which feels feminine towards the father. ⟨The bed-wetting is in this case a substitute for sexuality. Pressure of urine in dreams and also in the waking state is often an expression of some other pressure, for instance of fear, expectation, suppressed excitement, inability to speak, the need to express an unconscious content, etc. In our case the substitute for sexuality has the significance of a premature masculinity which is meant to compensate the inferiority of the child.

737   ⟨Although I do not intend to go into the psychology of

dreams in this connection, the motif of the black snake and of the black man should not pass unmentioned. Both these terrifying spectres threaten the dreamer as well as his mother. "Black" indicates something dark, the unconscious. The dream shows that the mother-child relationship is menaced by unconsciousness. The threatening agency is represented by the mythological motif of the "father animal"; in other words the father appears as threatening. This is in keeping with the tendency of the child to remain unconscious and infantile, which is decidedly dangerous. For the boy, the father is an anticipation of his own masculinity, conflicting with his wish to remain infantile. The snake's attack on the boy's face, the part that "sees," represents the danger to consciousness (blinding).⟩ [20]

738   This little example shows what goes on in the psyche of an eight-year-old child who is over-dependent on his parents, the blame for this lying partly on the too strict father and the too tender mother. ⟨The boy's identification with his mother and fear of his father are in this individual instance an infantile neurosis, but they represent at the same time the original human situation, the clinging of primitive consciousness to the unconscious, and the compensating impulse which strives to tear consciousness away from the embrace of the darkness. Because man has a dim premonition of this original situation behind his individual experience, he has always tried to give it generally valid expression through the universal motif of the divine hero's fight with the mother dragon, whose purpose is to deliver man from the power of darkness. This myth has a "saving," i.e., therapeutic significance, since it gives adequate expression to the dynamism underlying the individual entanglement. The myth is not to be causally explained as the consequence of a personal father-complex, but should be understood teleologically, as an attempt of the unconscious itself to rescue consciousness from the danger of regression. The ideas of "salvation" are not subsequent rationalizations of a father-complex; they are, rather,

[20] [*Orig.*: It is not difficult to see, from the Freudian standpoint, what the bed-wetting means in this case. Micturition dreams give us the clue. Here I would refer the reader to an analysis of this kind in my paper "The Analysis of Dreams" (cf. supra, pars. 82f.). Bed-wetting must be regarded as an infantile sexual substitute, and even in the dream-life of adults it is easily used as a cloak for the pressure of sexual desire.]

archetypally preformed mechanisms for the development of consciousness.⟩ 21

739   What we see enacted on the stage of world-history happens also in the individual. The child is guided by the power of the parents as by a higher destiny. But as he grows up, the struggle between his infantile attitude and his increasing consciousness begins. The parental influence, dating from the early infantile period, is repressed and sinks into the unconscious, but is not eliminated; by invisible threads it directs the apparently individual workings of the maturing mind. Like everything that has fallen into the unconscious, the infantile situation still sends up dim, premonitory feelings, feelings of being secretly guided by otherworldly influences. ⟨Normally these feelings are not referred back to the father, but to a positive or negative

21 [*Orig.:* The infantile attitude, it is evident, is nothing but infantile sexuality. If we now survey all the far-reaching possibilities of the infantile constellation, we are obliged to say that *in essence our life's fate is identical with the fate of our sexuality.* If Freud and his school devote themselves first and foremost to tracing out the individual's sexuality, it is certainly not in order to excite piquant sensations but to gain a deeper insight into the driving forces that determine the individual's fate. In this we are not saying too much, but rather understating the case. For, when we strip off the veils shrouding the problems of individual destiny, we at once widen our field of vision from the history of the individual to the history of nations. We can take a look, first of all, at the history of religion, at the history of the fantasy systems of whole peoples and epochs. The religion of the Old Testament exalted the paterfamilias into the Jehovah of the Jews, whom the people had to obey in fear and dread. The patriarchs were a stepping-stone to the Deity. The neurotic fear in Judaism, an imperfect or at any rate unsuccessful attempt at sublimation by a still too barbarous people, gave rise to the excessive severity of Mosaic law, the compulsive ceremonial of the neurotic.* Only the prophets were able to free themselves from it; for them the identifica-tion with Jehovah, complete sublimation, was successful. They became the fathers of the people. Christ, the fulfiller of their prophecies, put an end to this fear of God and taught mankind that the true relation to the Deity is love. Thus he destroyed the compulsive ceremonial of the law and was himself the exponent of the personal loving relationship to God. Later, the imperfect sublimations of the Christian Mass resulted once again in the ceremonial of the Church, from which only those of the numerous saints and reformers who were really capable of sublimation were able to break free. Not without cause, therefore, does modern theology speak of the liberating effect of "inner" or "personal" experience, for always the ardour of love transmutes fear and compulsion into a higher, freer type of feeling.

   [* *Orig. footnote:* Cf. Freud, *Zeitschrift für Religionspsychologie* (1907).] [I.e., "Obsessive Acts and Religious Practices."—EDITORS.]

deity. This change is accomplished partly under the influence of education, partly spontaneously. It is universal. Also, it resists conscious criticism with the force of an instinct, for which reason the soul (anima) may fittingly be described as naturaliter religiosa. The reason for this development, indeed its very possibility, is to be found in the fact that the child possesses an inherited system that anticipates the existence of parents and their influence upon him. In other words, behind the father stands the archetype of the father, and in this pre-existent archetype lies the secret of the father's power, just as the power which forces the bird to migrate is not produced by the bird itself but derives from its ancestors.

740   It will not have escaped the reader that the role which falls to the father-imago in our case is an ambiguous one. The threat it represents has a dual aspect: fear of the father may drive the boy out of his identification with the mother, but on the other hand it is possible that his fear will make him cling still more closely to her. A typically neurotic situation then arises: he wants and yet does not want, saying yes and no at the same time.

741   This double aspect of the father-imago is characteristic of the archetype in general: it is capable of diametrically opposite effects and acts on consciousness rather as Yahweh acted towards Job—ambivalently. And, as in the Book of Job, man is left to take the consequences. We cannot say with certainty that the archetype always acts in this way, for there are experiences which prove the contrary. But they do not appear to be the rule.) [22]

742   An instructive and well-known example of the ambivalent behaviour of the father-imago is the love-episode in the Book of Tobit.[23] Sara, the daughter of Raguel, of Ecbatana, desires to marry. But her evil fate wills it that seven times, one after the

---

[22] [Orig.: These are the roots of the first religious sublimations. In the place of the father with his constellating virtues and faults there appears on the one hand an altogether sublime deity, and on the other hand the devil, who in modern times has been largely whittled away by the realization of one's own moral responsibility. Sublime love is attributed to the former, low sexuality to the latter. As soon as we enter the field of neurosis, this antithesis is stretched to the limit. God becomes the symbol of the most complete sexual repression, the devil the symbol of sexual lust. Thus it is that the conscious expression of the father-constellation, like every expression of an unconscious complex when it appears in consciousness, acquires its Janus face, its positive and its negative components.]
[23] Chs. 3 : 7ff. and 8 : 1ff.

other, she chooses a husband who dies on the wedding-night. It is the evil spirit Asmodeus, by whom she is persecuted, that kills these men. She prays to Yahweh to let her die rather than suffer this shame again, for she is despised even by her father's maid-servants. The eighth bridegroom, her cousin Tobias, the son of Tobit, is sent to her by God. He too is led into the bridal chamber. Then old Raguel, who had only pretended to go to bed, goes out and thoughtfully digs his son-in-law's grave, and in the morning sends a maid to the bridal chamber to make sure that he is dead. But this time Asmodeus' role is played out, for Tobias is alive.

743   ⟨The story shows father Raguel in his two roles, as the inconsolable father of the bride and the provident digger of his son-in-law's grave. Humanly speaking he seems beyond reproach, and it is highly probable that he was. But there is still the evil spirit Asmodeus and his presence needs explaining. If we suspect old Raguel personally of playing a double role, this malicious insinuation would apply only to his sentiments; there is no evidence that he committed murder. These wicked deeds transcend the old man's daughter-complex as well as Sara's father-complex, for which reason the legend fittingly ascribes them to a demon. Asmodeus plays the role of a jealous father who will not give up his beloved daughter and only relents when he remembers his own positive aspect, and in that capacity at last gives Sara a pleasing bridegroom. He, significantly enough, is the eighth: the last and highest stage.[24] Asmodeus stands for the negative aspect of the father archetype, for the archetype is the genius and daemon of the personal human being, "the god of human nature, changeful of countenance, white and black." [25] The legend offers a psychologically correct explanation: it does not attribute superhuman evil to Raguel, it distinguishes between man and daemon, just as psychology must distinguish between what the human individual is and can do and what must be ascribed to the congenital, instinctual system, which the individual has not made but finds within him. We would be doing the gravest injustice to Raguel if we held

24 ⟨Cf. the axiom of Maria and the discussion of 3 and 4, 7 and 8, in *Psychology and Alchemy*, pars. 201ff. and 209.⟩

25 ⟨Horace, *Epistles*, II, 2, 187–89.⟩

him responsible for the fateful power of this system, that is, of the archetype.

744 ⟨The potentialities of the archetype, for good and evil alike, transcend our human capacities many times, and a man can appropriate its power only by identifying with the daemon, by letting himself be possessed by it, thus forfeiting his own humanity. The fateful power of the father complex comes from the archetype, and this is the real reason why the *consensus gentium* puts a divine or daemonic figure in place of the father. The personal father inevitably embodies the archetype, which is what endows his figure with its fascinating power. The archetype acts as an amplifier, enhancing beyond measure the effects that proceed from the father, so far as these conform to the inherited pattern.⟩ [26]

[26] [*Orig.:* Unfortunately medical etiquette forbids me to report a case of hysteria which fits this pattern exactly, except that there were not seven husbands but only three, unluckily chosen under all the ominous signs of an infantile constellation. Our first case, too, belongs to this category, and in our third case we see the old peasant at work, preparing to dedicate his daughter to a like fate.

[As a pious and dutiful daughter (cf. her prayer in Tobit, ch. 3), Sara has brought about the usual sublimation and splitting of the father-complex, on the one hand elevating her infantile love into the worship of God, and on the other turning the obsessive power of the father into the persecuting demon Asmodeus. The story is beautifully worked out and shows father Raguel in his two roles, as the inconsolable father of the bride and the provident digger of his son-in-law's grave, whose fate he foresees.

[This pretty fable has become a classic example in my analytical work, for we frequently meet with cases where the father-demon has laid his hand upon his daughter, so that her whole life long, even when she does marry, there is never a true inward union, because her husband's image never succeeds in obliterating the unconscious and continually operative infantile father-ideal. This is true not only of daughters, but also of sons. An excellent example of this kind of father-constellation can be found in Brill's recently published "Psychological Factors in Dementia Praecox" (1908).

[In my experience it is usually the father who is the decisive and dangerous object of the child's fantasy, and if ever it happened to be the mother I was able to discover behind her a grandfather to whom she belonged in her heart.

[I must leave this question open, because my findings are not sufficient to warrant a decision. It is to be hoped that experience in the years to come will sink deeper shafts into this obscure territory, on which I have been able to shed but a fleeting light, and will discover more about the secret workshop of the demon who shapes our fate, of whom Horace says:

"Scit Genius natale comes qui temperat astrum,
Naturae deus humanae, mortalis in unum,
Quodque caput, vultu mutabilis, albus et ater."]

71

THE PERSONAL AND THE COLLECTIVE
UNCONSCIOUS

Jung's idea that an archetypal image of masculine spirit lies at the core of an individual's father complex is given a convincing clinical demonstration in his account of a case.

---

202   In Freud's view, as most people know, the contents of the unconscious are reducible to infantile tendencies which are repressed because of their incompatible character. Repression is a process that begins in early childhood under the moral influence of the environment and continues throughout life. By means of analysis the repressions are removed and the repressed wishes made conscious.

203   According to this theory, the unconscious contains only those parts of the personality which could just as well be conscious, and have been suppressed only through the process of education. Although from one point of view the infantile tendencies of the unconscious are the most conspicuous, it would nonetheless be a mistake to define or evaluate the unconscious entirely in these terms. The unconscious has still another side to it: it includes not only repressed contents, but all psychic material that lies below the threshold of consciousness. It is impossible to explain the subliminal nature of all this material on the principle of repression, for in that case the removal of repression ought to endow a person with a prodigious memory which would thenceforth forget nothing.

204   We therefore emphatically affirm that in addition to the repressed material the unconscious contains all those psychic components that have fallen below the threshold, as well as sub-

liminal sense-perceptions. Moreover we know, from abundant experience as well as for theoretical reasons, that the unconscious also contains all the material that has *not yet* reached the threshold of consciousness. These are the seeds of future conscious contents. Equally we have reason to suppose that the unconscious is never quiescent in the sense of being inactive, but is ceaselessly engaged in grouping and regrouping its contents. This activity should be thought of as completely autonomous only in pathological cases; normally it is co-ordinated with the conscious mind in a compensatory relationship.

205   It is to be assumed that all these contents are of a personal nature in so far as they are acquired during the individual's life. Since this life is limited, the number of acquired contents in the unconscious must also be limited. This being so, it might be thought possible to empty the unconscious either by analysis or by making a complete inventory of the unconscious contents, on the ground that the unconscious cannot produce anything more than what is already known and assimilated into consciousness. We should also have to suppose, as already said, that if one could arrest the descent of conscious contents into the unconscious by doing away with repression, unconscious productivity would be paralysed. This is possible only to a very limited extent, as we know from experience. We urge our patients to hold fast to repressed contents that have been re-associated with consciousness, and to assimilate them into their plan of life. But this procedure, as we may daily convince ourselves, makes no impression on the unconscious, since it calmly goes on producing dreams and fantasies which, according to Freud's original theory, must arise from personal repressions. If in such cases we pursue our observations systematically and without prejudice, we shall find material which, although similar in form to the previous personal contents, yet seems to contain allusions that go far beyond the personal sphere.

206   Casting about in my mind for an example to illustrate what I have just said, I have a particularly vivid memory of a woman patient with a mild hysterical neurosis which, as we expressed it in those days [about 1910], had its principal cause in a "father-complex." By this we wanted to denote the fact that the patient's peculiar relationship to her father stood in her way. She had been on very good terms with her father, who had since

died. It was a relationship chiefly of feeling. In such cases it is usually the intellectual function that is developed, and this later becomes the bridge to the world. Accordingly our patient became a student of philosophy. Her energetic pursuit of knowledge was motivated by her need to extricate herself from the emotional entanglement with her father. This operation may succeed if her feelings can find an outlet on the new intellectual level, perhaps in the formation of an emotional tie with a suitable man, equivalent to the former tie. In this particular case, however, the transition refused to take place, because the patient's feelings remained suspended, oscillating between her father and a man who was not altogether suitable. The progress of her life was thus held up, and that inner disunity so characteristic of a neurosis promptly made its appearance. The so-called normal person would probably be able to break the emotional bond in one or the other direction by a powerful act of will, or else—and this is perhaps the more usual thing—he would come through the difficulty unconsciously, on the smooth path of instinct, without ever being aware of the sort of conflict that lay behind his headaches or other physical discomforts. But any weakness of instinct (which may have many causes) is enough to hinder a smooth unconscious transition. Then all progress is delayed by conflict, and the resulting stasis of life is equivalent to a neurosis. In consequence of the standstill, psychic energy flows off in every conceivable direction, apparently quite uselessly. For instance, there are excessive innervations of the sympathetic system, which lead to nervous disorders of the stomach and intestines; or the vagus (and consequently the heart) is stimulated; or fantasies and memories, uninteresting enough in themselves, become overvalued and prey on the conscious mind (mountains out of molehills). In this state a new motive is needed to put an end to the morbid suspension. Nature herself paves the way for this, unconsciously and indirectly, through the phenomenon of the transference (Freud). In the course of treatment the patient transfers the father-imago to the doctor, thus making him, in a sense, the father, and in the sense that he is *not* the father, also making him a substitute for the man she cannot reach. The doctor therefore becomes both a father and a kind of lover—in other words, an object of conflict. In him the opposites are united, and for this reason he stands for a quasi-

75

ideal solution of the conflict. Without in the least wishing it, he draws upon himself an over-valuation that is almost incredible to the outsider, for to the patient he seems like a saviour or a god. This way of speaking is not altogether so laughable as it sounds. It is indeed a bit much to be a father and lover at once. Nobody could possibly stand up to it in the long run, precisely because it is too much of a good thing. One would have to be a demigod at least to sustain such a role without a break, for all the time one would have to be the giver. To the patient in the state of transference, this provisional solution naturally seems ideal, but only at first; in the end she comes to a standstill that is just as bad as the neurotic conflict was. Fundamentally, nothing has yet happened that might lead to a real solution. The conflict has merely been transferred. Nevertheless a successful transference can—at least temporarily—cause the whole neurosis to disappear, and for this reason it has been very rightly recognized by Freud as a healing factor of first-rate importance, but, at the same time, as a provisional state only, for although it holds out the possibility of a cure, it is far from being the cure itself.

207   This somewhat lengthy discussion seemed to me essential if my example was to be understood, for my patient had arrived at the state of transference and had already reached the upper limit where the standstill begins to make itself disagreeable. The question now arose: what next? I had of course become the complete saviour, and the thought of having to give me up was not only exceedingly distasteful to the patient, but positively terrifying. In such a situation "sound common sense" generally comes out with a whole repertory of admonitions: "you simply must," "you really ought," "you just cannot," etc. So far as sound common sense is, happily, not too rare and not entirely without effect (pessimists, I know, exist), a rational motive can, in the exuberant feeling of buoyancy you get from the transference, release so much enthusiasm that a painful sacrifice can be risked with a mighty effort of will. If successful—and these things sometimes are—the sacrifice bears blessed fruit, and the erstwhile patient leaps at one bound into the state of being practically cured. The doctor is generally so delighted that he fails to tackle the theoretical difficulties connected with this little miracle.

208   If the leap does not succeed—and it did not succeed with my patient—one is then faced with the problem of resolving the

transference. Here "psychoanalytic" theory shrouds itself in a thick darkness. Apparently we are to fall back on some nebulous trust in fate: somehow or other the matter will settle itself. "The transference stops automatically when the patient runs out of money," as a slightly cynical colleague once remarked to me. Or the ineluctable demands of life make it impossible for the patient to linger on in the transference—demands which compel the involuntary sacrifice, sometimes with a more or less complete relapse as a result. (One may look in vain for accounts of such cases in the books that sing the praises of psychoanalysis!)

209　　To be sure, there are hopeless cases where nothing helps; but there are also cases that do not get stuck and do not inevitably leave the transference situation with bitter hearts and sore heads. I told myself, at this juncture with my patient, that there must be a clear and respectable way out of the impasse. My patient had long since run out of money—if indeed she ever possessed any—but I was curious to know what means nature would devise for a satisfactory way out of the transference deadlock. Since I never imagined that I was blessed with that "sound common sense" which always knows exactly what to do in every quandary, and since my patient knew as little as I, I suggested to her that we could at least keep an eye open for any movements coming from a sphere of the psyche uncontaminated by our superior wisdom and our conscious plannings. That meant first and foremost her dreams.

210　　Dreams contain images and thought-associations which we do not create with conscious intent. They arise spontaneously without our assistance and are representatives of a psychic activity withdrawn from our arbitrary will. Therefore the dream is, properly speaking, a highly objective, natural product of the psyche, from which we might expect indications, or at least hints, about certain basic trends in the psychic process. Now, since the psychic process, like any other life-process, is not just a causal sequence, but is also a process with a teleological orientation, we might expect dreams to give us certain *indicia* about the objective causality as well as about the objective tendencies, precisely because dreams are nothing less than self-representations of the psychic life-process.

211　　On the basis of these reflections, then, we subjected the dreams to a careful examination. It would lead too far to quote word for word all the dreams that now followed. Let it suffice to sketch their main character: the majority referred to the person of the doctor, that is to say, the actors were unmistakably the dreamer herself and her doctor. The latter, however, seldom appeared in his natural shape, but was generally distorted in a remarkable way. Sometimes his figure was of supernatural size, sometimes he seemed to be extremely aged, then again he resembled her father, but was at the same time curiously woven into nature, as in the following dream: *Her father (who in reality was of small stature) was standing with her on a hill that was covered with wheat-fields. She was quite tiny beside him, and he seemed to her like a giant. He lifted her up from the ground and held her in his arms like a little child. The wind swept over the wheat-fields, and as the wheat swayed in the wind, he rocked her in his arms.*

212   From this dream and from others like it I could discern various things. Above all I got the impression that her unconscious was holding unshakably to the idea of my being the father-lover, so that the fatal tie we were trying to undo appeared to be doubly strengthened. Moreover one could hardly avoid seeing that the unconscious placed a special emphasis on the supernatural, almost "divine" nature of the father-lover, thus accentuating still further the over-valuation occasioned by the transference. I therefore asked myself whether the patient had still not understood the wholly fantastic character of her transference, or whether perhaps the unconscious could never be reached by understanding at all, but must blindly and idiotically pursue some nonsensical chimera. Freud's idea that the unconscious can "do nothing but wish," Schopenhauer's blind and aimless Will, the gnostic demiurge who in his vanity deems himself perfect and then in the blindness of his limitation creates something lamentably imperfect—all these pessimistic suspicions of an essentially negative background to the world and the soul came threateningly near. And there would indeed be nothing to set against this except a well-meaning "you ought," reinforced by a stroke of the axe that would cut down the whole phantasmagoria for good and all.

213   But, as I turned the dreams over and over in my mind, there dawned on me another possibility. I said to myself: it cannot be denied that the dreams continue to speak in the same old meta-

phors with which our conversations have made the patient as well as myself sickeningly familiar. But the patient has an undoubted understanding of her transference fantasy. She knows that I appear to her as a semi-divine father-lover, and she can, at least intellectually, distinguish this from my factual reality. Therefore the dreams are obviously reiterating the conscious standpoint minus the conscious criticism, which they completely ignore. They reiterate the conscious contents, not *in toto,* but insist on the fantastic standpoint as opposed to "sound common sense."

214   I naturally asked myself what was the source of this obstinacy and what was its purpose? That it must have some purposive meaning I was convinced, for there is no truly living thing that does not have a final meaning, that can in other words be explained as a mere left-over from antecedent facts. But the energy of the transference is so strong that it gives one the impression of a vital instinct. That being so, what is the purpose of such fantasies? A careful examination and analysis of the dreams, especially of the one just quoted, revealed a very marked tendency— in contrast to conscious criticism, which always seeks to reduce things to human proportions—to endow the person of the doctor with superhuman attributes. He had to be gigantic, primordial, huger than the father, like the wind that sweeps over the earth— was he then to be made into a god? Or, I said to myself, was it rather the case that the unconscious was trying to *create* a god out of the person of the doctor, as it were to free a vision of God from the veils of the personal, so that the transference to the person of the doctor was no more than a misunderstanding on the part of the conscious mind, a stupid trick played by "sound common sense"? Was the urge of the unconscious perhaps only apparently reaching out towards the person, but in a deeper sense towards a god? Could the longing for a god be a *passion* welling up from our darkest, instinctual nature, a passion unswayed by any outside influences, deeper and stronger perhaps than the love for a human person? Or was it perhaps the highest and truest meaning of that inappropriate love we call "transference," a little bit of real *Gottesminne,* that has been lost to consciousness ever since the fifteenth century?

215   No one will doubt the reality of a passionate longing for a human person; but that a fragment of religious psychology, an

historical anachronism, indeed something of a medieval curiosity—we are reminded of Mechtild of Magdeburg—should come to light as an immediate living reality in the middle of the consulting-room, and be expressed in the prosaic figure of the doctor, seems almost too fantastic to be taken seriously.

216   A genuinely scientific attitude must be unprejudiced. The sole criterion for the validity of an hypothesis is whether or not it possesses an heuristic—i.e., explanatory—value. The question now is, can we regard the possibilities set forth above as a valid hypothesis? There is no *a priori* reason why it should not be just as possible that the unconscious tendencies have a goal beyond the human person, as that the unconscious can "do nothing but wish." Experience alone can decide which is the more suitable hypothesis. This new hypothesis was not entirely plausible to my very critical patient. The earlier view that I was the father-lover, and as such presented an ideal solution of the conflict, was incomparably more attractive to her way of feeling. Nevertheless her intellect was sufficiently keen to appreciate the theoretical possibility of the new hypothesis. Meanwhile the dreams continued to disintegrate the person of the doctor and swell him to ever vaster proportions. Concurrently with this there now occurred something which at first I alone perceived, and with the utmost astonishment, namely a kind of subterranean undermining of the transference. Her relations with a certain friend deepened perceptibly, notwithstanding the fact that consciously she still clung to the transference. So that when the time came for leaving me, it was no catastrophe, but a perfectly reasonable parting. I had the privilege of being the only witness during the process of severance. I saw how the transpersonal control-point developed—I cannot call it anything else—a *guiding function* and step by step gathered to itself all the former personal over-valuations; how, with this afflux of energy, it gained influence over the resisting conscious mind without the patient's consciously noticing what was happening. From this I realized that the dreams were not just fantasies, but self-representations of unconscious developments which allowed the psyche of the patient gradually to grow out of the pointless personal tie.[1]

217   This change took place, as I showed, through the unconscious development of a transpersonal control-point; a virtual

---

[1] Cf. the "transcendent function" in *Psychological Types*, Def. 51, "Symbol."

goal, as it were, that expressed itself symbolically in a form which can only be described as a vision of God. The dreams swelled the human person of the doctor to superhuman proportions, making him a gigantic primordial father who is at the same time the wind, and in whose protecting arms the dreamer rests like an infant. If we try to make the patient's conscious, and traditionally Christian, idea of God responsible for the divine image in the dreams, we would still have to lay stress on the distortion. In religious matters the patient had a critical and agnostic attitude, and her idea of a possible deity had long since passed into the realm of the inconceivable, i.e., had dwindled into a complete abstraction. In contrast to this, the god-image of the dreams corresponded to the archaic conception of a nature-daemon, something like Wotan. Θεὸς τὸ πνεῦμα, 'God is spirit,' is here translated back into its original form where πνεῦμα means 'wind': God is the wind, stronger and mightier than man, an invisible breath-spirit. As in Hebrew *ruah*, so in Arabic *ruh* means breath and spirit.[2] Out of the purely personal form the dreams develop an archaic god-image that is infinitely far from the conscious idea of God. It might be objected that this is simply an infantile image, a childhood memory. I would have no quarrel with this assumption if we were dealing with an old man sitting on a golden throne in heaven. But there is no trace of any sentimentality of that kind; instead, we have a primordial idea that can correspond only to an archaic mentality.

218   These primordial ideas, of which I have given a great many examples in my *Symbols of Transformation*, oblige one to make, in regard to unconscious material, a distinction of quite a different character from that between "preconscious" and "unconscious" or "subconscious" and "unconscious." The justification for these distinctions need not be discussed here. They have their specific value and are worth elaborating further as points of view. The fundamental distinction which experience has forced upon me claims to be no more than that. It should be evident from the foregoing that we have to distinguish in the unconscious a layer which we may call the *personal unconscious*. The materials contained in this layer are of a personal nature in so far as they have the character partly of acquisitions derived

2 For a fuller elaboration of this theme see *Symbols of Transformation*, index, s.v. "wind."

from the individual's life and partly of psychological factors which could just as well be conscious. It can readily be understood that incompatible psychological elements are liable to repression and therefore become unconscious. But on the other hand this implies the possibility of making and keeping the repressed contents conscious once they have been recognized. We recognize them as personal contents because their effects, or their partial manifestation, or their source can be discovered in our personal past. They are the integral components of the personality, they belong to its inventory, and their loss to consciousness produces an inferiority in one respect or another—an inferiority, moreover, that has the psychological character not so much of an organic lesion or an inborn defect as of a lack which gives rise to a feeling of moral resentment. The sense of moral inferiority always indicates that the missing element is something which, to judge by this feeling about it, really ought not be missing, or which could be made conscious if only one took sufficient trouble. The moral inferiority does not come from a collision with the generally accepted and, in a sense, arbitrary moral law, but from the conflict with one's own self which, for reasons of psychic equilibrium, demands that the deficit be redressed. Whenever a sense of moral inferiority appears, it indicates not only a need to assimilate an unconscious component, but also the possibility of such assimilation. In the last resort it is a man's moral qualities which force him, either through direct recognition of the need or indirectly through a painful neurosis, to assimilate his unconscious self and to keep himself fully conscious. Whoever progresses along this road of self-realization must inevitably bring into consciousness the contents of the personal unconscious, thus enlarging the scope of his personality. I should add at once that this enlargement has to do primarily with one's moral consciousness, one's knowledge of oneself, for the unconscious contents that are released and brought into consciousness by analysis are usually unpleasant—which is precisely why these wishes, memories, tendencies, plans, etc. were repressed. These are the contents that are brought to light in much the same way by a thorough confession, though to a much more limited extent. The rest comes out as a rule in dream analysis. It is often very interesting to watch how the dreams fetch up the essential points, bit by bit and with the nicest choice.

The total material that is added to consciousness causes a considerable widening of the horizon, a deepened self-knowledge which, more than anything else, one would think, is calculated to humanize a man and make him modest. But even self-knowledge, assumed by all wise men to be the best and most efficacious, has different effects on different characters. We make very remarkable discoveries in this respect in practical analysis, but I shall deal with this question in the next chapter.

²¹⁹ As my example of the archaic idea of God shows, the unconscious seems to contain other things besides personal acquisitions and belongings. My patient was quite unconscious of the derivation of "spirit" from "wind," or of the parallelism between the two. This content was not the product of her thinking, nor had she ever been taught it. The critical passage in the New Testament was inaccessible to her—τὸ πνεῦμα πνεῖ ὅπου ϑέλει —since she knew no Greek. If we must take it as a wholly personal acquisition, it might be a case of so-called cryptomnesia,[3] the unconscious recollection of a thought which the dreamer had once read somewhere. I have nothing against such a possibility in this particular case; but I have seen a sufficient number of other cases—many of them are to be found in the book mentioned above—where cryptomnesia can be excluded with certainty. Even if it were a case of cryptomnesia, which seems to me very improbable, we should still have to explain what the predisposition was that caused just this image to be retained and later, as Semon puts it, "ecphorated" (ἐκφορεῖν, Latin *efferre,* 'to produce'). In any case, cryptomnesia or no cryptomnesia, we are dealing with a genuine and thoroughly primitive god-image that grew up in the unconscious of a civilized person and produced a living effect—an effect which might well give the psychologist of religion food for reflection. There is nothing about this image that could be called personal: it is a wholly collective image, the ethnic origin of which has long been known to us. Here is an historical image of world-wide distribution that has come into existence again through a natural psychic function. This is not so very surprising, since my patient was born into the

---

[3] Cf. Flournoy, *Des Indes à la planète Mars: Étude sur un cas de somnambulisme avec glossolalie* (trans. by D. B. Vermilye as *From India to the Planet Mars*), and Jung, "Psychology and Pathology of So-called Occult Phenomena," pars. 138ff.

world with a human brain which presumably still functions today much as it did of old. We are dealing with a reactivated
archetype, as I have elsewhere called these primordial images.[4]
These ancient images are restored to life by the primitive, ana-
logical mode of thinking peculiar to dreams. It is not a question
of inherited ideas, but of inherited thought-patterns.[5]

220   In view of these facts we must assume that the unconscious
contains not only personal, but also impersonal collective components in the form of inherited categories[6] or archetypes. I
have therefore advanced the hypothesis that at its deeper levels
the unconscious possesses collective contents in a relatively active state. That is why I speak of a collective unconscious.

[4] Cf. *Psychological Types,* Def. 26.
[5] Consequently, the accusation of "fanciful mysticism" levelled at my ideas is
lacking in foundation.
[6] Hubert and Mauss, *Mélanges d'histoire des religions,* p. xxix.

IV. LOGOS AND EROS; SOL AND LUNA

THE PERSONIFICATION OF THE OPPOSITES
THE MOON NATURE

Jung's attempt to equate Logos and Eros, his intuitive conceptions
of masculine and feminine consciousness, with the alchemical Sol
and Luna is only partly successful; there is more than "discrimination, judgement and insight" to Sol and more, certainly, than
"the capacity to relate" to Luna. These stereotyped conceptions are
of most use when applied to the unconscious of men and women,
where the character of the opposite sex appears in a caricatured,
archetypal way. Jung comments wryly that in a man the lunar anima and in a woman the solar animus has the greatest influence
upon consciousness.

---

224   For purely psychological reasons I have, in other of my writings, tried to equate the masculine consciousness with the concept of Logos and the feminine with that of Eros. By Logos I
meant discrimination, judgment, insight, and by Eros I meant
the capacity to relate. I regarded both concepts as intuitive ideas
which cannot be defined accurately or exhaustively. From the
scientific point of view this is regrettable, but from a practical
one it has its value, since the two concepts mark out a field of
experience which it is equally difficult to define.

225   As we can hardly ever make a psychological proposition without immediately having to reverse it, instances to the contrary
leap to the eye at once: men who care nothing for discrimination, judgment, and insight, and women who display an almost
excessively masculine proficiency in this respect. I would like to
describe such cases as the regular exceptions. They demonstrate,
to my mind, the common occurrence of a psychically predomi-

nant contrasexuality. Wherever this exists we find a forcible intrusion of the unconscious, a corresponding exclusion of the consciousness specific to either sex, predominance of the shadow and of contrasexuality, and to a certain extent even the presence of symptoms of possession (such as compulsions, phobias, obsessions, automatisms, exaggerated affects, etc.). This inversion of roles is probably the chief psychological source for the alchemical concept of the hermaphrodite. In a man it is the lunar anima, in a woman the solar animus, that influences consciousness in the highest degree. Even if a man is often unaware of his own anima-possession, he has, understandably enough, all the more vivid an impression of the animus-possession of his wife, and vice versa.

226   Logos and Eros are intellectually formulated intuitive equivalents of the archetypal images of Sol and Luna. In my view the two luminaries are so descriptive and so superlatively graphic in their implications that I would prefer them to the more pedestrian terms Logos and Eros, although the latter do pin down certain psychological peculiarities more aptly than the rather indefinite "Sol and Luna." The use of these images requires at any rate an alert and lively fantasy, and this is not an attribute of those who are inclined by temperament to purely intellectual concepts. These offer us something finished and complete, whereas an archetypal image has nothing but its naked fullness, which seems inapprehensible by the intellect. Concepts are coined and negotiable values; images are life.

THE PERSONIFICATION OF THE OPPOSITES

1. INTRODUCTION

104   The alchemist's endeavours to unite the opposites culminate in the "chymical marriage," the supreme act of union in which the work reaches its consummation. After the hostility of the four elements has been overcome, there still remains the last and most formidable opposition, which the alchemist expressed very aptly as the relationship between male and female. We are inclined to think of this primarily as the power of love, of passion, which drives the two opposite poles together, forgetting that such a vehement attraction is needed only when an equally strong resistance keeps them apart. Although enmity was put only between the serpent and the woman (Genesis 3 : 15), this curse nevertheless fell upon the relationship of the sexes in general. Eve was told: "Thy desire shall be to thy husband, and he shall rule over thee." And Adam was told: "Cursed is the ground for thy sake . . . because thou hast hearkened unto the voice of thy wife" (3 : 16f.). Primal guilt lies between them, an *interrupted state of enmity,* and this appears unreasonable only to our rational mind but not to our psychic nature. Our reason is often influenced far too much by purely physical considerations, so that the union of the sexes seems to it the only sensible thing and the urge for union the most sensible instinct of all. But if we conceive of nature in the higher sense as the totality of all phenomena, then the physical is only one of her aspects, the other is pneumatic or spiritual. The first has always been regarded as feminine, the second as masculine. The goal of the one is union, the goal of the other is discrimination. Because it overvalues the physical, our contemporary reason lacks spiritual orientation, that is, pneuma. The alchemists seem to have had an inkling of this, for how otherwise could they have come upon that strange myth of the country of the King of the Sea, where

only like pairs with like and the land is unfruitful?[1] It was obviously a realm of innocent friendship, a kind of paradise or golden age, to which the "Philosophers," the representatives of the physical, felt obliged to put an end with their good advice. But what happened was not by any means a natural union of the sexes; on the contrary it was a "royal" incest, a sinful deed that immediately led to imprisonment and death and only afterwards restored the fertility of the country. As a parable the myth is certainly ambiguous; like alchemy in general, it can be understood spiritually as well as physically, "tam moralis quam chymica."[2] The physical goal of alchemy was gold, the panacea, the elixir of life; the spiritual one was the rebirth of the (spiritual) light from the darkness of Physis: healing self-knowledge and the deliverance of the pneumatic body from the corruption of the flesh.

105   A subtle feature of the "Visio Arislei" is that the very one who is meditating a pairing of the sexes is king of the land of innocence. Thus the *rex marinus* says: "Truly I have a son and a daughter, and therefore I am king over my subjects, because they possess nothing of these things. Yet I have borne a son and a daughter in my brain."[3] Hence the king is a potential traitor to the paradisal state of innocence because he can generate "in his head," and he is king precisely because he is capable of this sin against the previous state of innocence. Since he can be different from them he is *more* than any of his subjects and therefore rightly their king, although, from the physical standpoint, he is counted a bad ruler.[4]

106   Here again we see the contrast between alchemy and the prevailing Christian ideal of attempting to restore the original state of innocence by monasticism and, later, by the celibacy of the priesthood. The conflict between worldliness and spirituality, latent in the love-myth of Mother and Son, was elevated by Christianity to the mystic marriage of sponsus (Christ) and sponsa (Church), whereas the alchemists transposed it to the physical plane as the coniunctio of Sol and Luna. The Christian solution of the conflict is purely pneumatic, the physical rela-

[1] "Visio Arislei," *Art. aurif.*, I, pp. 146ff.
[2] Maier, *Symb. aur. mensae*, p. 156.   [3] "Visio Arislei," p. 147.
[4] The philosophers say to him: "Lord, king you may be, but you rule and govern badly." *

tions of the sexes being turned into an allegory or—quite illegitimately—into a sin that perpetuates and even intensifies the original one in the Garden. Alchemy, on the other hand, exalted the most heinous transgression of the law, namely incest, into a symbol of the union of opposites, hoping in this way to bring back the golden age. For both trends the solution lay in extrapolating the union of sexes into another medium: the one projected it into the spirit, the other into matter. But neither of them located the problem in the place where it arose—the soul of man.

107   No doubt it would be tempting to assume that it was more convenient to shift such a supremely difficult question on to another plane and then represent it as having been solved. But this explanation is too facile, and is psychologically false because it supposes that the problem was asked consciously, found to be painful, and consequently moved on to another plane. This stratagem accords with our modern way of thinking but not with the spirit of the past, and there are no historical proofs of any such neurotic operation. Rather does all the evidence suggest that the problem has always seemed to lie outside the psyche as known to us. Incest was the hierosgamos of the gods, the mystic prerogative of kings, a priestly rite, etc. In all these cases we are dealing with an archetype of the collective unconscious which, as consciousness increased, exerted an ever greater influence on conscious life. It certainly seems today as if the ecclesiastical allegories of the bridegroom and bride, not to mention the now completely obsolete alchemical coniunctio, had become so faded that one meets with incest only in criminology and the psychopathology of sex. Freud's discovery of the Oedipus complex, a special instance of the incest problem in general, and its universal incidence have, however, reactivated this ancient problem, though mostly only for doctors interested in psychology. Even though laymen know very little about certain medical anomalies or have a wrong idea of them, this does not alter the facts any more than does the layman's ignorance of the actual percentage of cases of tuberculosis or psychosis.

108   Today the medical man knows that the incest problem is practically universal and that it immediately comes to the surface when the customary illusions are cleared away from the foreground. But mostly he knows only its pathological side and

leaves it steeped in the odium of its name, without learning the lesson of history that the painful secret of the consulting-room is merely the embryonic form of a perennial problem which, in the suprapersonal sphere of ecclesiastical allegory and in the early phases of natural science, created a symbolism of the utmost importance. Generally he sees only the "materia vilis et in via eiecta" from the pathological side and has no idea of its spiritual implications. If he saw this, he could also perceive how the spirit that has disappeared returns in each of us in unseemly, indeed reprehensible guise, and in certain predisposed cases causes endless confusion and destruction in great things as in small. The psychopathological problem of incest is the aberrant, natural form of the union of opposites, a union which has either never been made conscious at all as a psychic task or, if it was conscious, has once more disappeared from view.

109   The persons who enact the drama of this problem are man and woman, in alchemy King and Queen, Sol and Luna. In what follows I shall give an account of the way in which alchemy describes the symbolic protagonists of the supreme opposition.

2. SOL

110   In alchemy, the sun signifies first of all gold, whose sign it shares. But just as the "philosophical" gold is not the "common" gold,[5] so the sun is neither just the metallic gold [6] nor the heavenly orb.[7] Sometimes the sun is an active substance hidden in the gold and is extracted as the *tinctura rubea* (red tincture). Sometimes, as the heavenly body, it is the possessor of magically effective and transformative rays. As gold and a heavenly body [8]

5 Senior, *De chemia*, p. 92.*

6 "Gold and silver in their metallic form are not the matter of our stone." * "Tractatus aureus," *Mus. herm.*, p. 32 (Waite, I, p. 33).

7 Because gold is not subject to oxidization, Sol is an arcanum described in the "Consilium coniugii" as follows: "A substance equal, permanent, fixed for the length of eternity" * (*Ars chemica*, p. 58). "For Sol is the root of incorruption." * "Verily there is no other foundation of the Art than the sun and its shadow" * (ibid., p. 138).

8 Rupescissa, *La Vertu et la propriété de la quinte essence*, p. 19: "Jceluy soleil est vray or. . . . L'or de Dieu est appelé par les Philosophes, Soleil; car il est fils du Soleil du Ciel, et est engendré par les influences du Soleil ès entrailles et veines de la terre."

it contains an active sulphur of a red colour, hot and dry.[9] Because of this red sulphur the alchemical sun, like the corresponding gold, is red.[10] As every alchemist knew, gold owes its red colour to the admixture of Cu (copper), which he interpreted as Kypris (the Cyprian, Venus), mentioned in Greek alchemy as the transformative substance.[11] Redness, heat, and dryness are the classical qualities of the Egyptian Set (Gk. Typhon), the evil principle which, like the alchemical sulphur, is closely connected with the devil. And just as Typhon has his kingdom in the forbidden sea, so the sun, as *sol centralis*, has its sea, its "crude perceptible water," and as *sol coelestis* its "subtle imperceptible water." This sea water (*aqua pontica*) is extracted from sun and moon. Unlike the Typhonian sea, the life-giving power of this water is praised, though this does not mean that it is invariably good.[12] It is the equivalent of the two-faced Mercurius, whose poisonous nature is often mentioned. The Typhonian aspect of the active sun-substance, of the red sulphur, of the water "that does not make the hands wet," [13] and of the "sea water" should not be left out of account. The author of the "Novum lumen chemicum" cannot suppress a reference to the latter's paradoxical nature: "Do not be disturbed because you sometimes find contradictions in my treatises, after the custom of the philosophers; these are necessary, if you understand that no rose is found without thorns." [14]

111   The active sun-substance also has favourable effects. As the so-called "balsam" it drips from the sun and produces lemons, oranges, wine, and, in the mineral kingdom, gold.[15] In man the

9 Sulphur is even identical with fire. Cf. "Consil. coniugii" (*Ars chemica*, p. 217): "Know therefore that sulphur is fire, that is, Sol." * In Mylius (*Phil. ref.*, p. 185) Sol is identical with sulphur, i.e., the alchemical Sol signifies the active substance of the sun or of the gold.

10 "Our Sol is ruddy and burning." * (Zacharius, "Opusculum," *Theatr. chem.*, I, p. 840.) Bernardus Trevisanus goes so far as to say: "Sol is nothing other than sulphur and quicksilver." * (Ibid., Flamel's annotations, p. 860.)

11 Olympiodorus (Berthelot, *Alch. grecs*, II, iv, 43): "Smear [with it] the leaves of the shining goddess, the red Cyprian."

12 Cf. the sulphur parable (infra par. 144), where the water is "most dangerous."

13 Hoghelande, *Theatr. chem.*, I, p. 181.

14 *Mus. herm.*, pp. 581f. (Waite, II, p. 107).

15 Steeb, *Coelum sephiroticum*, p. 50. Paracelsus, in "De natura rerum" (Sudhoff, XI, p. 330), says: "Now the life of man is none other than an astral balsam, a balsamic impression, a heavenly and invisible fire, an enclosed air." *De Vita longa*

balsam forms the "radical moisture, from the sphere of the supracelestial waters"; it is the "shining" or "lucent body" which "from man's birth enkindles the inner warmth, and from which come all the motions of the will and the principle of all appetition." It is a "vital spirit," and it has "its seat in the brain and its governance in the heart." [16]

112   In the "Liber Platonis Quartorum," a Sabaean treatise, the *spiritus animalis* or solar sulphur is still a πνεῦμα πάρεδρον, a ministering spirit or familiar who can be conjured up by magical invocations to help with the work. [17]

113   From what has been said about the active sun-substance it should be clear that Sol in alchemy is much less a definite chemical substance than a "virtus," a mysterious power [18] believed to have a generative [19] and transformative effect. Just as the physical sun lightens and warms the universe, so, in the human body, there is in the heart a sunlike arcanum from which life and warmth stream forth. [20] "Therefore Sol," says Dorn, "is rightly named the first after God, and the father and begetter of all, [21] because in him the seminal and formal virtue of all things whatsoever lies hid." [22] This power is called "sulphur." [23] It is a hot, daemonic principle of life, having the closest affinities with the sun in the earth, the "central fire" or "ignis gehennalis" (fire of

---

(ed. Bodenstein, fol. c 7ᵛ): "(Treating of a certain invisible virtue) he calls it balsam, surpassing all bodily nature, which preserves the two bodies by conjunction, and upholds the celestial body together with the four elements." *

[16] Steeb, p. 117. The moon draws "universal form and natural life" from the sun. (Dorn, "Physica genesis," *Theatr. chem.*, I, p. 397.)

[17] *Theatr. chem.*, V. p. 130.

[18] "It were vain to believe, as many do, that the sun is merely a heavenly fire." * (Dorn, "Physica Trismegisti," *Theatr. chem.*, I, p. 423.)

[19] The alchemists still believed with Proclus that the sun generates the gold. Cf. Proclus, *Commentaries on the Timaeus of Plato* 18 B (trans. by Taylor), I, p. 36.

[20] Dorn ("Phys. Trismeg.," p. 423) says: "As the fount of life of the human body, it is the centre of man's heart, or rather that secret thing which lies hid within it, wherein the natural heat is active." *

[21] Zosimos (Berthelot, *Alch. grecs*, III, xxi, 3) cites the saying of Hermes: "The sun is the maker of all things." *

[22] "Phys. Trismeg.," p. 423.* The Codex Berol. Lat. 532 (fol. 154ᵛ) says of the germ-cell of the egg: "The sun-point, that is, the germ of the egg, which is in the yolk." *

[23] "The first and most powerful male and universal seed is, by its nature, sulphur, the first and most powerful cause of all generation. Wherefore Paracelsus says that the sun and man through man generate man." * (Dorn, ibid.)

hell). Hence there is also a *Sol niger,* a black sun, which coincides with the *nigredo* and *putrefactio,* the state of death.[24] Like Mercurius, Sol in alchemy is ambivalent.

114   The miraculous power of the sun, says Dorn, is due to the fact that "all the simple elements are contained in it, as they are in heaven and in the other heavenly bodies." "We say that the sun is a single element," he continues, tacitly identifying it with the quintessence. This view is explained by a remarkable passage from the "Consilium coniugii": "The Philosophers maintained that the father of the gold and silver is the animating principle [*animal*] of earth and water, or man or part of a man, such as hair, blood, menstruum, etc." [25] The idea at the back of this is that primitive conception of a universal power of growth, healing, magic, and prestige,[26] which is to be found as much in the sun as in men and plants, so that not only the sun but man too, and especially the enlightened man, the adept, can generate the gold by virtue of this universal power. It was clear to Dorn (and to other alchemists as well) that the gold was not made by the usual chemical procedures,[27] for which reason he called gold-making (chrysopoeia) a "miracle." The miracle was performed by a *natura abscondita* (hidden nature), a metaphysical entity "perceived not with the outward eyes, but solely by the mind." [28] It was "infused from heaven,[29] provided that the adept had approached as closely as possible to things divine and

24 Cf. infra, p. 98. The alchemical sun also rises out of the darkness of the earth, as in *Aurora Consurgens*, pp. 125f.: "This earth made the moon . . . then the sun arose . . . after the darkness which thou hast appointed therein before the sunrise." *

25 *Ars chemica*, p. 158. On a primitive level, blood is the seat of the soul. Hair signifies strength and divine power. (Judges 13 : 5 and 16 : 17ff.)

26 Cf. the works of Lehmann, Preuss, and Röhr. A collection of mana-concepts can be found in my "On Psychic Energy," pars. 114ff.

27 Cf. Bonus, "Pretiosa margarita novella," *Theatr. chem.,* V, p. 648: "And in this wise Alchemy is supernatural, and is divine. And in this stone is all the difficulty of the Art, nor can any sufficient natural reason be adduced why this should be so. And thus it is when the intellect cannot comprehend this nor satisfy itself, but must yet believe it, as in miraculous divine matters; even as the foundation of the Christian faith, being supernatural, must first be taken as true by unbelievers, because its end is attained miraculously and supernaturally. Therefore God alone is the operator, nature taking no part in the work." *

28 "Spec. phil.," *Theatr. chem.,* I, p. 298; also "Phil. chemica," p. 497.

29 Cf. *Aurora Consurgens*, p. 111: "For I could not wonder enough at the great virtue of the thing, which is bestowed upon and infused into it from heaven." *

at the same time had extracted from the substances the subtlest powers "fit for the miraculous act." "There is in the human body a certain aethereal substance, which preserves its other elemental parts and causes them to continue," [30] he says. This substance or virtue is hindered in its operations by the "corruption of the body"; but "the Philosophers, through a kind of divine inspiration, knew that this virtue and heavenly vigour can be freed from its fetters, not by its contrary . . . but by its like." [31] Dorn calls it "veritas." "It is the supreme power, an unconquerable fortress, which hath but very few friends, and is besieged by innumerable enemies." It is "defended by the immaculate Lamb," and signifies the heavenly Jerusalem in the inner man. "In this fortress is the true and indubitable treasure, which is not eaten into by moths, nor dug out by thieves, but remaineth for ever, and is taken hence after death." [32]

115   For Dorn, then, the spark of divine fire implanted in man becomes what Goethe in his original version of *Faust* called Faust's "entelechy," which was carried away by the angels. This supreme treasure "the animal man understandeth not. . . . We are made like stones, having eyes and seeing not." [33]

116   After all this, we can say that the alchemical Sol, as a "certain luminosity" (*quaedam luminositas*), is in many respects equal to the *lumen naturae*. This was the real source of illumination in alchemy, and from alchemy Paracelsus borrowed this same source in order to illuminate the art of medicine. Thus the concept of Sol has not a little to do with the growth of modern consciousness, which in the last two centuries has relied more and more on the observation and experience of natural objects. Sol therefore seems to denote an important psychological fact. Consequently, it is well worth while delineating its peculiarities in greater detail on the basis of the very extensive literature.

117   Generally Sol is regarded as the masculine and active half of Mercurius, a supraordinate concept whose psychology I have discussed in a separate study. [34] Since, in his alchemical form,

30 "Phil. meditativa," *Theatr. chem.*, I, p. 456. There is a similar passage on p. 457: "Further, in the human body is concealed a certain substance of heavenly nature, known to very few, which needeth no medicament, being itself the incorrupt medicament." *   31 P. 457.
32 P. 458. See also "Spec. phil.," p. 266.
33 P. 459.*
34 "The Spirit Mercurius."

Mercurius does not exist in reality, he must be an unconscious projection, and because he is an absolutely fundamental concept in alchemy he must signify the unconscious itself. He is by his very nature the unconscious, where nothing can be differentiated; but, as a *spiritus vegetativus* (living spirit), he is an active principle and so must always appear in reality in differentiated form. He is therefore fittingly called "duplex," both active and passive. The "ascending," active part of him is called Sol, and it is only through this that the passive part can be perceived. The passive part therefore bears the name of Luna, because she borrows her light from the sun.[35] Mercurius demonstrably corresponds to the cosmic Nous of the classical philosophers. The human mind is a derivative of this and so, likewise, is the diurnal life of the psyche, which we call consciousness.[36] Consciousness requires as its necessary counterpart a dark, latent, non-manifest side, the unconscious, whose presence can be known only by the light of consciousness.[37] Just as the day-star rises out of the nocturnal sea, so, ontogenetically and phylogenetically, consciousness is born of unconsciousness and sinks back every night to this primal condition. This duality of our psychic life is the prototype and archetype of the Sol-Luna symbolism. So much did the alchemist sense the duality of his unconscious assumptions that, in the face of all astronomical evidence, he equipped the sun with a shadow: "The sun and its shadow bring the work to perfection." [38] Michael Maier, from whom this saying is taken, avoids the onus of explanation by substituting the shadow of the earth for the shadow of the sun in the forty-fifth discourse of his *Scrutinium*. Evidently he could

35 Cf. the ancient idea that the sun corresponds to the right eye and the moon to the left. (Olympiodorus in Berthelot, *Alch. grecs*, II, iv, 51.)

36 Just as for the natural philosophers of the Middle Ages the sun was the god of the physical world, so the "little god of the world" is consciousness.

37 Consciousness, like the sun, is an "eye of the world." (Cf. Pico della Mirandola, "Disputationes adversus astrologos," lib. III, cap. X, p. 88r.) In his *Heptaplus* (Expositio 7, cap. IV, p. 11r) he says: "Since Plato calls the Sun . . . the visible son of God, why do we not understand that we are the image of the invisible son? And if he is the true light enlightening every mind, he hath as his most express image this Sun, which is the light of the image enlightening every body." *

38 This idea occurs already in the *Turba* (ed. by Ruska, p. 130): "But he who hath tinged the poison of the sages with the sun and its shadow, hath attained to the greatest secret." * Mylius (*Phil. ref.*, p. 22) says: "In the shadow of the sun is the heat of the moon." *

not wholly shut his eyes to astronomical reality. But then he cites the classical saying of Hermes: "Son, extract from the ray its shadow," [39] thus giving us clearly to understand that the shadow is contained in the sun's rays and hence could be extracted from them (whatever that might mean). Closely related to this saying is the alchemical idea of a black sun, often mentioned in the literature.[40] This notion is supported by the self-evident fact that without light there is no shadow, so that, in a sense, the shadow too is emitted by the sun. For this physics requires a dark object interposed between the sun and the observer, a condition that does not apply to the alchemical Sol, since occasionally it appears as black itself. It contains both light and darkness. "For what, in the end," asks Maier, "is this sun without a shadow? The same as a bell without a clapper." While Sol is the most precious thing, its shadow is *res vilissima* or *quid vilius alga* (more worthless than seaweed). The antinomian thinking of alchemy counters every position with a negation and vice versa. "Outwardly they are bodily things, but inwardly they are spiritual," says Senior.[41] This view is true of all alchemical qualities, and each thing bears in itself its opposite.[42]

118   To the alchemical way of thinking the shadow is no mere *privatio lucis;* just as the bell and its clapper are of a tangible substantiality, so too are light and shadow. Only thus can the saying of Hermes be understood. In its entirety it runs: "Son,

39 From ch. II of the "Tractatus aureus," *Ars chemica*, p. 15.*
40 Cf. Mylius, *Phil. ref.*, p. 19. Here the *sol niger* is synonymous with the *caput corvi* and denotes the *anima media natura* in the state of *nigredo*, which appears when the "earth of the gold is dissolved by its own proper spirit." * Psychologically, this means a provisional extinction of the conscious standpoint owing to an invasion from the unconscious. Mylius refers to the "ancient philosophers" as a source for the *sol niger*. A similar passage occurs on p. 118: "The sun is obscured at its birth. And this denigration is the beginning of the work, the sign of putrefaction, and the sure beginning of the commixture." * This *nigredo* is the "changing darkness of purgatory." Ripley (*Chymische Schrifften*, p. 51) speaks of a "dark" sun, adding: "You must go through the gate of the blackness if you would gain the light of Paradise in the whiteness." Cf. *Turba*, p. 145: "nigredo solis."
41 *De chemia*, p. 91.*
42 The *sol niger* is a "counter-sun," just as there is an invisible sun enclosed in the centre of the earth. (See Agnostus, *Prodromus Rhodostauroticus*, 1620, Vr.) A similar idea is found in Ventura (*Theatr. chem.*, II, p. 276): "And as at the beginning the sun is hidden in the Moon, so, hidden at the end, it is extracted from the moon." *

extract from the ray its shadow, and the corruption that arises from the mists which gather about it, befoul it and veil its light; for it is consumed by necessity and by its redness."[43] Here the shadow is thought of quite concretely; it is a mist that is capable not only of obscuring the sun but of befouling it ("coinquinare" —a strong expression). The redness (*rubedo*) of the sun's light is a reference to the red sulphur in it, the active burning principle, destructive in its effects. In man the "natural sulphur," Dorn says, is identical with an "elemental fire" which is the "cause of corruption," and this fire is "enkindled by an invisible sun unknown to many, that is, the sun of the Philosophers." The natural sulphur tends to revert to its first nature, so that the body becomes "sulphurous" and fitted to receive the fire that "corrupts man back to his first essence."[44] The sun is evidently an instrument in the physiological and psychological drama of return to the prima materia, the death that must be undergone if man is to get back to the original condition of the simple elements and attain the incorrupt nature of the pre-worldly paradise. For Dorn this process was spiritual and moral as well as physical.

119   Sol appears here in a dubious, indeed a "sulphurous" light: it corrupts, obviously because of the sulphur it contains.[45]

120   Accordingly, Sol is the transformative substance, the prima materia as well as the gold tincture. The anonymous treatise "De arte chymica" distinguishes two parts or stages of the lapis. The first part is called the *sol terrenus* (earthly sun). "Without

43 "Tractatus aureus," *Ars chemica*, p. 15.

44 Dorn, "Spec. phil.," *Theatr. chem.*, I, p. 308. He conceives it in the first place as a physiologically destructive action which turns the salts in the body into chalk, so that the body becomes "sulphurous." But this medical observation is introduced by the remark: "Because man is engendered in corruption, his own substance pursues him with hatred." By this he means original sin and the corruption resulting therefrom.

45 I am not forgetting that the dangerous quality of Sol may also be due to the fact that his rays contain the miraculous water "which by the power of the magnet is extracted from the rays of the sun and moon." * This water is a putrefying agent, because "before it is properly cooked it is a deadly poison." Mylius, *Phil. ref.*, p. 314. This aqua permanens is the ὕδωρ θεῖον (divine water), the "divinity" being sulphur. It was called "sulphur water" (τὸ θεῖον also means sulphur) and is the same as mercury. Θεῖον or θήϊον in Homer was believed to possess apotropaic powers, and this may be the reason why it was called "divine."

the earthly sun, the work is not perfected." [46] In the second part of the work Sol is joined with Mercurius.

On earth these stones are dead, and they do nothing unless the activity of man is applied to them. [Consider] [47] the profound analogy of the gold: the aethereal heaven was locked to all men, so that all men had to descend into the underworld, where they were imprisoned for ever. But Christ Jesus unlocked the gate of the heavenly Olympus and threw open the realm of Pluto, that the souls might be freed, when the Virgin Mary, with the cooperation of the Holy Ghost in an unutterable mystery and deepest sacrament, conceived in her virgin womb that which was most excellent in heaven and upon earth, and finally bore for us the Redeemer of the whole world, who by his overflowing goodness shall save all who are given up to sin, if only the sinner shall turn to him. But the Virgin remained incorrupt and inviolate: therefore not without good reason is Mercurius made equal [aequiparatur] to the most glorious and worshipful Virgin Mary. [48]

It is evident from this that the coniunctio of Sol and Mercurius is a hierosgamos, with Mercurius playing the role of bride. If one does not find this analogy too offensive, one may ask oneself with equanimity whether the arcanum of the opus alchymicum, as understood by the old masters, may not indeed be considered an equivalent of the dogmatic mystery. For the psychologist the decisive thing here is the subjective attitude of the alchemist. As I have shown in *Psychology and Alchemy,* such a profession of faith is by no means unique. [49]

[121]   The metaphorical designation of Christ as Sol [50] in the language of the Church Fathers was taken quite literally by the alchemists and applied to their *sol terrenus.* When we remember that the alchemical Sol corresponds psychologically to consciousness, the diurnal side of the psyche, we must add the Christ analogy to this symbolism. Christ appears essentially as the *son*—the son of his mother-bride. The role of the son does in fact devolve upon ego-consciousness since it is the offspring of the maternal

[46] *Art. aurif.,* I, p. 58ff.*

[47] The text only has "auri similitudinem profundam," without a verb.

[48] *Art. aurif.,* I, pp. 58off.   [49] "The Lapis-Christ Parallel."

[50] Especially as "sol iustitiae" (sun of justice), Malachi 4 : 2. Cf. Honorius of Autun, *Speculum de mysteriis Ecclesiae* (Migne, *P.L.,* vol. 172, col. 921): "For, like to the sun beneath a cloud, so did the sun of justice lie concealed under human flesh." * Correspondingly, the Gnostic Anthropos is identical with the sun. (Cf. Reitzenstein, *Poimandres,* p. 280.)

unconscious. Now according to the arch authority, the "Tabula smaragdina," Sol is the father of Mercurius, who in the above quotation appears as feminine and as the mother-bride. In that capacity Mercurius is identical with Luna, and—via the Luna-Mary-Ecclesia symbolism—is equated with the Virgin. Thus the treatise "Exercitationes in Turbam" says: "As blood is the origin of flesh, so is Mercurius the origin of Sol . . . and thus Mercurius is Sol and Sol is Mercurius." [51] Sol is therefore father and son at once, and his feminine counterpart is mother and daughter in one person; furthermore, Sol and Luna are merely aspects of the same substance that is simultaneously the cause and the product of both, namely Mercurius duplex, of whom the philosophers say that he contains everything that is sought by the wise. This train of thought is based on a quaternity:

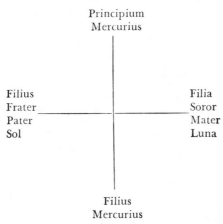

```
                    Principium
                    Mercurius
                        |
                        |
                        |
   Filius                          Filia
   Frater _____ Soror
   Pater                           Mater
   Sol                             Luna
                        |
                        |
                        |
                     Filius
                    Mercurius
```

122   Although the Sol symbolism is reminiscent of the dogmatic models, its basic schema is very different; for the dogmatic schema is a Trinity embracing only the Deity but not the universe.[52] The alchemical schema appears to embrace only the material world, yet, on account of its quaternary character, it comes near to being a representation of totality as exemplified in the symbol of the cross erected between heaven and earth. The cross is by implication the Christian totality symbol: as an instrument of torture it expresses the sufferings on earth of the

[51] *Art. aurif.*, I, p. 155.
[52] The alchemical equivalent of the Trinity is the three-headed serpent (**Mercurius**). See *Psychology and Alchemy*, fig. 54.

incarnate God, and as a quaternity it expresses the universe, which also includes the material world. If we now add to this cruciform schema the four protagonists of the divine world-drama—the Father as *auctor rerum*, the Son, his counterpart the Devil (to fight whom he became man), and the Holy Ghost, we get the following quaternity:

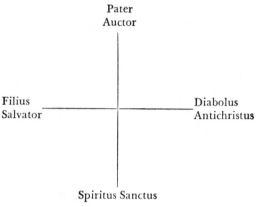

Pater
Auctor

Filius   Diabolus
Salvator   Antichristus

Spiritus Sanctus

123   I will not discuss the various aspects of this quaternity more closely here, as I have already done so in a separate study.[53] I mention it only for comparison with the alchemical one. Quaternities such as these are logical characteristics of Gnostic thinking, which Koepgen has aptly called "circular."[54] We have

---

[53] Cf. my "Psychological Approach to the Dogma of the Trinity," pars. 243ff. Though some may find it objectionable, the opposition between Christ and the devil in the above schema presupposes an inner relationship (regarded by the Ebionites, says Epiphanius, as that between two brothers). Angelus Silesius seems to have felt something of the sort, too:

"Were from the Devil all his His-ness gone,
You'd see the Devil sitting in God's throne."

Cherubinischer Wandersmann, I, No. 143 (Cf. Flitch version, p. 144). By "His-ness" Angelus Silesius means the "selfhood which damns," as is incontestably true of all selfhood that does not acknowledge its identity with God.

[54] The thinking in the Psalms and of the prophets is "circular. Even the Apocalypse consists of spiral images . . . One of the main characteristics of Gnostic thinking is circularity." (Koepgen, *Gnosis des Christentums*, p. 149.) Koepgen gives an example from Ephraem Syrus: "Make glad the body through the soul, but give the soul back to the body, that both may be glad that after the separation they are joined again" (p. 151). An alchemist could have said the same of the uroboros, since this is the primal symbol of alchemical truth. Koepgen also describes dogma as "circular": it is "round in the sense of a living reality. . . . Dogmas are con-

already met similar figures in our account of the opposites, which were often arranged in quaternities. The rhythm of both schemas is divided into three steps:

Alchemical:	{ Beginning Origin Mercurius }	—— { Development Sol Luna }	—— { Goal Filius Mercurius
Christian:	{ Auctor Pater }	—— { Development of Conflict Salvator Diabolus }	—— { Paraclete Holy Ghost Church or King- dom of God

124   The alchemical drama leads from below upwards, from the darkness of the earth to the winged, spiritual *filius macrocosmi* and to the *lux moderna;* the Christian drama, on the other hand, represents the descent of the Kingdom of Heaven to earth. One has the impression of a mirror-world, as if the God-man coming down from above—as in the Gnostic legend—were reflected in the dark waters of Physis. The relation of the unconscious to the conscious mind is to a certain extent complementary, as elementary psychogenic symptoms and dreams caused by simple somatic stimuli prove.[55] (Hence the strange idea, taught for instance by Rudolf Steiner, that the Hereafter possesses qualities complementary to those of this world.) Careful observation and analysis show, however, that not all dreams can be regarded mechanically as mere complementary devices but must be interpreted rather as attempts at *compensation*, though this does not prevent very many dreams from having, on a superficial view, a distinct complementary character. Similarly, we could regard the alchemical movement as a reflection of the Christian one.[56]

cerned with the religious reality, and this is circular" (p. 52). He calls attention to the "fact of not knowing and not recognizing, which lies at the core of the dogma itself" (p. 51). This remark indicates the reason or one of the reasons for the "roundness": dogmas are approximative concepts for a fact that exists yet cannot be described, and can only be approached by circumambulation. At the same time, these facts are "spheres" of indeterminable extent, since they represent *principles*. Psychologically they correspond to the archetypes. Overlapping and interpenetration are an essential part of their nature. "Roundness" is a peculiarity not only of dogmas, but, in especial degree, of alchemical thought.

55 Particularly dreams about hunger, thirst, pain, and sex. Another complementary factor is the feminine nature of the unconscious in a man.

56 For the compensatory aspect of this "reflection" see *Psychology and Alchemy*, pars. 26ff.

Koepgen makes a significant distinction between two aspects of Christ: the descending, incarnate God, and the ascending, Gnostic Christ who returns to the Father. We cannot regard the latter as the same as the alchemical *filius regius,* although Koepgen's schema offers an exact parallel to the alchemical situation.[57] The redeemer figure of alchemy is not commensurable with Christ. Whereas Christ is God and is begotten by the Father, the *filius regius* is the soul of nature, born of the world-creating Logos, of the Sapientia Dei sunk in matter. The *filius regius* is also a son of God, though of more distant descent and not begotten in the womb of the Virgin Mary but in the womb of Mother Nature: he is a "third sonship" in the Basilidian sense.[58] No traditional influences should be invoked in considering the conceptual structure of this filius; he is more an autochthonous product deriving from an unconscious, logical development of trends which had already reached the field of consciousness in the early Christian era, impelled by the same unconscious necessity as produced the later development of ideas. For, as our modern experience has shown, the collective unconscious is a living process that follows its own inner laws and gushes up like a spring at the appointed time. That it did so in alchemy in such an obscure and complicated way was due essentially to the great psychological difficulties of antinomian thinking, which continually came up against the demand for the logical consistency of the metaphysical figures, and for their emotional absoluteness. The "bonum superexcedens" of God allows no integration of evil. Although Nicholas Cusanus ventured the bold thought of the *coincidentia oppositorum,* its logical consequence—the relativity of the God-concept—proved disastrous for

57 Koepgen, p. 112.

58 Cf. "The Spirit Mercurius," pars. 282f. In another respect, also, the *filius philosophorum* is a "third" when we consider the development in the concept of the devil among the Ebionites (Epiphanius, *Panarium*, XXX). They spoke of two figures begotten by God, one of them Christ, the other the devil. The latter, according to Psellus, was called by the Euchites Satanaël, the elder brother of Christ. (Cf. *Aion*, par. 229, and "The Spirit Mercurius," pars. 271f. In relation to these two the *filius regius*—as *donum Spiritus Sancti* and son of the prima materia—is a "third sonship," which, in common with the prima materia, can trace its descent—though a more distant one—from God. For the threefold sonship see Hippolytus, *Elenchos*, VII, 22, 7f. (Legge, II, pp. 71f.) and *Aion*, pars. 118f. The "sonships" come from the "true light" (John 1 : 9), from the Logos, the *sapientia Patris.* Hippolytus, VII, 22, 4 (Legge, II, pp. 68f.).

Angelus Silesius, and only the withered laurels of the poet lie on his grave. He had drunk with Jacob Boehme at the fount of Mater Alchimia. The alchemists, too, became choked in their own confusions.

125   Once again, therefore, it is the medical investigators of nature who, equipped with new means of knowledge, have rescued these tangled problems from projection by making them the proper subject of psychology. This could never have happened before, for the simple reason that there was no psychology of the unconscious. But the medical investigator, thanks to his knowledge of archetypal processes, is in the fortunate position of being able to recognize in the abstruse and grotesque-looking symbolisms of alchemy the nearest relatives of those serial fantasies which underlie the delusions of paranoid schizophrenia as well as the healing processes at work in the psychogenic neuroses. The overweening contempt which other departments of science have for the apparently negligible psychic processes of "pathological individuals" should not deter the doctor in his task of helping and healing the sick. But he can help the sick psyche only when he meets it as the unique psyche of that particular individual, and when he knows its earthly and unearthly darknesses. He should also consider it just as important a task to defend the standpoint of consciousness, clarity, "reason," and an acknowledged and proven good against the raging torrent that flows for all eternity in the darkness of the psyche—a πάντα ῥεῖ that leaves nothing unaltered and ceaselessly creates a past that can never be retrieved. He knows that there is nothing purely good in the realm of human experience, but also that for many people it is better to be convinced of an absolute good and to listen to the voice of those who espouse the superiority of consciousness and unambiguous thinking. He may solace himself with the thought that one who can join the shadow to the light is the possessor of the greater riches. But he will not fall into the temptation of playing the law-giver, nor will he pretend to be a prophet of the truth: for he knows that the sick, suffering, or helpless patient standing before him is not the public but is Mr or Mrs X, and that the doctor has to put something tangible and helpful on the table or he is no doctor. His duty is always to the individual, and he is persuaded that nothing has happened if this individual has not been helped. He is answerable

to the individual in the first place and to society only in the second. If he therefore prefers individual treatment to collective ameliorations, this accords with the experience that social and collective influences usually produce only a mass intoxication, and that only man's action upon man can bring about a real transformation.[59]

126   It cannot have escaped the alchemists that their Sol had something to do with man. Thus Dorn says: "From the beginning man was sulphur." Sulphur is a destructive fire "enkindled by the invisible sun," and this sun is the Sol Philosophorum,[60] which is the much sought-after and highly praised philosophic gold, indeed the goal of the whole work.[61] In spite of the fact that Dorn regards the sun and its sulphur as a kind of physiological component of the human body, it is clear that we are dealing with a piece of physiological mythology, i.e., a projection.

127   In the course of our inquiry we have often seen that, despite the complete absence of any psychology, the alchemical projections sketch a picture of certain fundamental psychological facts and, as it were, reflect them in matter. One of these fundamental facts is the primary pair of opposites, consciousness and unconsciousness, whose symbols are Sol and Luna.

128   We know well enough that the unconscious appears personified: mostly it is the anima [62] who in singular or plural form represents the collective unconscious. The personal unconscious is personified by the shadow.[63] More rarely, the collective unconscious is personified as a Wise Old Man.[64] (I am speaking here

[59] In psychotherapy the situation is no different from what it is in somatic medicine, where surgery is performed on the *individual*. I mention this fact because of the modern tendency to treat the psyche by group analysis, as if it were a collective phenomenon. The psyche as an individual factor is thereby eliminated.
[60] "Spec. phil.," *Theatr. chem.,* I, p. 308.
[61] Ripley, *Chymische Schrifften,* p. 34: "For then your Work will obtain the perfect whiteness. Then turn from the East towards midday, there it should rest at a fiery place, for that is the harvest or end of the Work. . . . Thereupon the sun will shine pure red in its circle and will triumph after the darkness."
[62] Cf. "Concerning the Archetypes, with Special Reference to the Anima Concept." An example of the anima in plural form is given in *Psychology and Alchemy,* pars. 58ff.
[63] Examples of both archetypes are to be found ibid., Part II. Cf. also *Aion,* chs. 2 and 3. Another problem is the *shadow of the self,* which is not considered here.
[64] Cf. *Psychology and Alchemy,* par. 159.

only of masculine psychology, which alone can be compared with that of the alchemists.) It is still rarer for Luna to represent the nocturnal side of the psyche in dreams. But in the products of active imagination the symbol of the moon appears much more often, as also does the sun, which represents the luminous realm of the psyche and our diurnal consciousness. The modern unconscious has little use for sun and moon as dream-symbols.[65] Illumination ("a light dawns," "it is becoming clear," etc.) can be expressed just as well or even better in modern dreams by switching on the electric light.

129   It is therefore not surprising if the unconscious appears in projected and symbolized form, as there is no other way by which it might be perceived. But this is apparently not the case with consciousness. Consciousness, as the essence of all conscious contents, seems to lack the basic requirements for a projection. Properly understood, projection is not a voluntary happening; it is something that approaches the conscious mind from "outside," a kind of sheen on the object, while all the time the subject remains unaware that he himself is the source of light which causes the cat's eye of the projection to shine. Luna is therefore conceivable as a projection; but Sol as a projection, since it symbolizes consciousness, seems at first glance a contradiction in terms, yet Sol is no less a projection than Luna. For just as we perceive nothing of the real sun but light and heat and, apart from that, can know its physical constitution only by inference, so our consciousness issues from a dark body, the ego, which is the indispensable condition for all consciousness, the latter being nothing but the association of an object or a content with the ego. The ego, ostensibly the thing we know most about, is in fact a highly complex affair full of unfathomable obscurities. Indeed, one could even define it as a *relatively constant personification of the unconscious itself,* or as the Schopenhauerian mirror in which the unconscious becomes aware of its own face.[66] All the worlds that have ever existed before man were

65 Examples of the sun and moon dreams are given ibid., p. 135.

66 Here the concept of the *self* can be mentioned only in passing. (For a detailed discussion see *Aion,* ch. 4.) The self is the hypothetical summation of an indescribable totality, one half of which is constituted by ego-consciousness, the other by the shadow. The latter, so far as it can be established empirically, usually presents itself as the inferior or negative personality. It comprises that part of the collective unconscious which intrudes into the personal sphere, there forming the so-called

physically *there*. But they were a nameless happening, not a definite actuality, for there did not yet exist that minimal concentration of the psychic factor, which was also present, to speak the word that outweighed the whole of Creation: That is the world, and this is I! That was the first morning of the world, the first sunrise after the primal darkness, when that inchoately conscious complex, the ego, the son of the darkness, knowingly sundered subject and object, and thus precipitated the world and itself into definite existence,[67] giving it and itself a voice and a name. The refulgent body of the sun is the ego and its field of consciousness—*Sol et eius umbra:* light without and darkness within. In the source of light there is darkness enough for any amount of projections, for the ego grows out of the darkness of the psyche.

130 In view of the supreme importance of the ego in bringing reality to light, we can understand why this infinitesimal speck in the universe was personified as the sun, with all the attributes that this image implies. As the medieval mind was incomparably more alive than ours to the divine quality of the sun, we may assume that the totality character of the sun-image was implicit in all its allegorical or symbolic applications. Among the sig-

---

personal unconscious. The shadow forms, as it were, the bridge to the figure of the anima, who is only partly personal, and through her to the impersonal figures of the collective unconscious. The concept of the self is essentially intuitive and embraces ego-consciousness, shadow, anima, and collective unconscious in indeterminable extension. As a totality, the self is a coincidentia oppositorum; it is therefore bright and dark and yet neither.

If we hypostatize the self and derive from it (as from a kind of pre-existent personality) the ego and the shadow, then these would appear as the empirical aspects of the opposites that are preformed in the self. Since I have no wish to construct a world of speculative concepts, which leads merely to the barren hair-splitting of philosophical discussion, I set no particular store by these reflections. If such concepts provisionally serve to put the empirical material in order, they will have fulfilled their purpose. The empiricist has nothing to say about the concepts self and God in themselves, and how they are related to one another.

67 Genesis 1 : 1–7 is a projection of this process. The coming of consciousness is described as an objective event, the active subject of which is not the ego but Elohim. Since primitive people very often do not feel themselves the subject of their thinking, it is possible that in the distant past consciousness appeared as an outside event that happened to the ego, and that it was integrated with the subject only in later times. Illumination and inspiration, which in reality are sudden expansions of consciousness, still seem to have, even for us, a subject that is not the ego. Cf. Neumann, *The Origins and History of Consciousness,* pp. 102ff.

nifications of the sun as totality the most important was its frequent use as a God-image, not only in pagan times but in the sphere of Christianity as well.

131   Although the alchemists came very close to realizing that the ego was the mysteriously elusive arcane substance and the longed-for lapis, they were not aware that with their sun symbol they were establishing an intimate connection between God and the ego. As already remarked, projection is not a voluntary act; it is a natural phenomenon beyond the interference of the conscious mind and peculiar to the nature of the human psyche. If, therefore, it is this nature that produces the sun symbol, nature herself is expressing an identity of God and ego. In that case only unconscious nature can be accused of blasphemy, but not the man who is its victim. It is the rooted conviction of the West that God and the ego are worlds apart. In India, on the other hand, their identity was taken as self-evident. It was the nature of the Indian mind to become aware of the world-creating significance of the consciousness [68] manifested in man.[69] The West, on the contrary, has always emphasized the littleness, weakness, and sinfulness of the ego, despite the fact that it elevated one man to the status of divinity. The alchemists at least suspected man's hidden godlikeness, and the intuition of Angelus Silesius finally expressed it without disguise.

132   The East resolves these confusing and contradictory aspects by merging the ego, the personal atman, with the universal atman and thus explaining the ego as the veil of Maya. The Western alchemist was not consciously aware of these problems. But when his unspoken assumptions and his symbols reached the plane of conscious gnosis, as was the case with Angelus

[68] I use the word "consciousness" here as being equivalent to "ego," since in my view they are aspects of the same phenomenon. Surely there can be no consciousness without a knowing subject, and vice versa.

[69] Cf. Rig-Veda, X, 31, 6 (trans. from Deussen, *Geschichte der Philosophie*, I, 1, p. 140):

"And this prayer of the singer, continually expanding,
Became a cow that was there before the world was,
The gods are foster-children of the same brood,
Dwelling together in the womb of this god."

Vajasaneyi-samhita, 34, 3 (trans. from Deussen, *Die Geheimlehre des Veda*, p. 17):

"He who as consciousness, thought, decision,
Dwells as immortal light within man."

Silesius, it was precisely the littleness and lowliness of the ego [70] that impelled him to recognize its identity with its extreme opposite.[71] It was not the arbitrary opinions of deranged minds that gave rise to such insights, but rather the nature of the psyche itself, which, in East and West alike, expresses these truths either directly or clothed in transparent metaphors. This is understandable when we realize that a world-creating quality attaches to human consciousness as such. In saying this we violate no religious convictions, for the religious believer is at liberty to regard man's consciousness (through which, as it were, a second world-creation was enacted) as a divine instrument.

133   I must point out to the reader that these remarks on the significance of the ego might easily prompt him to charge me with grossly contradicting myself. He will perhaps remember that he has come across a very similar argument in my other writings. Only there it was not a question of ego but of the *self,* or rather, of the personal atman in contradistinction and in relation to the suprapersonal atman. I have defined the self as the totality of the conscious and the unconscious psyche, and the ego as the central reference-point of consciousness. It is an essential part of the self, and can be used *pars pro toto* when the significance of consciousness is borne in mind. But when we want to lay emphasis on the psychic totality it is better to use the term "self." There is no question of a contradictory definition, but merely of a difference of standpoint.

[70] "Save as a child, one goes not in where all
    God's children are: the door is much too small."
                    Cherubinischer Wandersmann, I, No. 153.
[71] "I am God's child and son, and he is mine.
    How comes it that we both can both combine?" (I, 256)
    "God is my centre when I close him in;
    And my circumference when I melt in him." (III, 148)
    "God, infinite, more present is in me
    Than if a sponge should soak up all the sea." (IV, 156)
    "The hen contains the egg, the egg the hen,
    The twain in one, and yet the one in twain." (IV, 163)
    "God becomes 'I' and takes my manhood on:
    Because I was before him was that done!" (IV, 259)

V. THE MASCULINE IN WOMEN

Anonymous

[ORIGINAL IN ENGLISH]

Dear Dr. N.,   12 November 1957

What you told me is a typical story of what I call the projection of the anima into a woman and of the animus into a man. Anima is the soul-image of a man, represented in dreams or fantasies by a feminine figure. It symbolizes the function of relationship. The animus is the image of spiritual forces in a woman, symbolized by a masculine figure. If a man or a woman is unconscious of these inner forces, they appear in a projection.

The psychiatrist calls you "his equal," and that feeling of relationship shows that you carry the image of his soul. Since he is unable to see you as a real woman behind his projection, you seem to be a "sphinx." In reality his soul is his sphinx, and he should try to solve the riddle.

You are wrong in assuming that he alone needs help. You need help as well. You call yourself a woman of a "very ordinary intellectual capacity" who has "never delved very deep into any metaphysical subject." As your story shows, the projection of the animus into a "psychiatrist of international repute" happened because you should get more psychological knowledge. Knowing more about the soul and its mysteries you could free yourself from the fascination which makes you suffer. In the second half of life one should begin to get acquainted with the inner world. That is a general problem.

Your world seemed to be a happy one. But the strange happenings showed that something ought to be changed.

The projection of anima and animus causes mutual fascination. Phenomena which you describe as "telepathic" happen when one gets emotional, i.e., when the unconscious has an opportunity to enter consciousness. You really ought to know a bit more about the psychology of the unconscious. It would help you to understand the situation, which—by the way—should be understood. There is a little book by Frieda Fordham: *Introduction to Jung's Psychology* (Pelican Books), which I recommend to you.

Faithfully yours, C. G. JUNG

☐ A woman, M.D., in England.

THE HOUSTON FILMS

So you see, when you have lived in primitive conditions, in the primeval forest among primitive people, you know that phenomenon. You are seized by a spell, and then you do something that is unexpected. Several times when I was in Africa I got into such situations and afterwards I was amazed. One day I was in the Sudan, and it was really a very dangerous situation which I didn't recognize at the moment at all. But I was seized by a spell, and I did something I wouldn't have expected, I couldn't have invented it. The archetype is a force. It has an autonomy and it can suddenly seize you. It is like a seizure. Falling in love at first sight is something like that. You see, you have a certain image in yourself, without knowing it, of woman, of *the* woman. Then you see that girl, or at least a good imitation of your type, and instantly you get a seizure and you are gone. And afterwards you may discover that it was a hell of a mistake. A man is quite able, he is intelligent enough, to see that the woman of his "choice," as one says, was no choice, he has been caught! He sees that she is no good at all, that she is a hell of a business, and he tells me so. He says, "For God's sake, doctor, help me to get rid of that woman!" He can't, though, he is like clay in her fingers. That is the archetype, the archetype of the anima.[9] And he thinks it is all his soul, you know! It's the same with the girls. When a man sings very high, a girl thinks he must have a very wonderful spiritual character because he can sing the high C, and she is badly disappointed when she marries that particular number. Well, that's the archetype of the animus.

[9] For the anima see *Two Essays on Analytical Psychology,* CW 7, pars. 296ff.; "Concerning the Archetypes, with Special Reference to the Anima Concept," CW 9 i; *Aion,* CW 9 ii, ch. III.

FROM ESTHER HARDING'S
NOTEBOOKS: 1922, 1925

4 July

I began by describing how I always had so much to say before I got into the room, so that I had to edit my thoughts because of the many undertones of meaning. Jung agreed that my language was scanty, and yet he felt it to be full of allusion. Extraverts' language is thin and poor, but profuse, so that although what they want to say may be very slight, at least when they have finished they have said what they set out to say. He went on to say that when speaking to an extravert he has to cut down his thoughts; also when he is speaking to an introvert he has to cut down, for the thought of an introvert, even if expanded into a book, would not be fully expressed. . . .

I had been trying to find out the meaning of my [slip of the tongue] and thought it was in protest against the extra difficulty of the feminine position regarding searching for the anima. This he denied. He said a man must take up a feminine attitude, while a woman must fight her animus, a masculine attitude. I asked, "Is this why I always want to fight you?" And he replied, "In so far as I am your animus. As far as you are identified to your animus, so far will you project him to me. And then, if you battle me with him who is demonic, I call *my* demon, my anima, to my aid, and it is two married couples fighting. Then you have a hell of a row." He said this is what happens when you get a reciprocal transference. But that as he is not [word illegible], I need not fear that would happen to him.

Then he began talking about how it happens that a professional woman lives her animus. The professional situation is new for woman and needs a new adaptation, and this, as always, is readily supplied by the animus. On the other hand, analysis requires a new adaptation from a man, for to sit still and patiently try to understand a woman's mind is far from a masculine attitude. The only time he does it is as lover to his mistress; he will not do so for his wife, for she is only his wife. In love, his anima shows him how. He then takes on a feminine tenderness and uses the baby talk he learned from his mother; he calls on the eternal image of the feminine in himself. But [in analysis] that won't do. [The male analyst] has got to learn the feminineness of a man, which is not the anima. He must not let his masculinity be overwhelmed, or his weakness calls out the animus in the woman patient.

Similarly, the professional woman takes on the animus, the prototype of the father, and develops a god-almightiness, [an imitation of] the hero, instead of developing the masculinity of the female. This animus is *primitive* man, and men want to react to it with their fists. But, as this is a woman, that way is barred to them; so they shun her—just as a man who lives his anima is shunned by all really womanly women.

Dr. Jung went on to speak of the strength of womanhood, how it is stronger than any [imitation of the] male adaptation, and how a woman who is woman from the crown of her head to the tip of her toe can afford to be masculine, just as a man who is sure of his masculinity can afford to be tender and patient like a woman. . . .

Next he spoke of the Self and how it can be separated off from the demons. He reiterated that words in the realm of the spirit are creative and full of power. I said "You mean as *Logos?*" He replied, "Yes. God spake and created from the chaos—and here we are all gods for ourselves. But use few words here, words that you are sure of. Do not make a long theory or you will entangle yourself in a net, in a trap."

Next he spoke of fear. He said, "Be afraid of the world, for it is big and strong; and fear the demons within, for they are many and brutal; but do not fear yourself, for that is your Self." I said I feared to open the door for fear the demons would come out and destroy. He said, "If you lock them up they will as surely destroy. The only way of delimiting the Self is by experiment. Go as far as your desire goes, and you will presently find that you have gone as far as your own laws allow. If you feel afraid, be brave enough to run away. Find a hole to hide in, for this is the action of a brave man, and by so doing you are exercising courage. Presently the swing of cowardice will be over, and courage will take its place." I said, "But how hopelessly unstable and changeable you will appear!" He replied, "Then be unstable. A new stability will reassert itself. Does one live for other people or for oneself? Here is the place where one must learn true unselfishness."

The law was made by man. We made it. It is therefore below us, and we can be above it. As St. Paul said, "I am redeemed and am freed from the law." He realized that, as man, he had made it. So also a contract cannot bind us, for we who made it can break it.

Thus, vice too, if entered into sincerely as a means of finding and expressing the Self, is not vice, for the fearless honesty cuts that out. But when we are bound by an artificial barrier, or by laws and moralities that have entered into us, then we are prevented from finding, or even from seeing, that there is a real barrier of the Self outside this artificial barrier. We fear that if we break through this artificial barrier we shall find ourselves in limitless space. But within each of us is the *self-regulating Self.*

5 July

I began the hour by telling Jung how something wonderful had happened to me yesterday, that his talk on the animus relationship had cleared things up, so that much had clicked into place, and that now I felt quite different. I said that yesterday we were dealing with the negative relationship to the animus, but there must also be a positive relationship. He replied that there certainly must—but that the important part of analysis was to get that negative point cleared, for that is the growing point of differentiation from the unconscious. Until that is clear, the voice of the animus is as the voice of God within us; in any case, we respond to it as if it were. When we are not aware of the negative aspect of the animus, we are still animal, still connected to nature, therefore unconscious and less than human. We need to reach a higher degree of consciousness, which must be sought at *that* point. Then we discover a new country. And it is our responsibility to cultivate it. ("To him that knoweth to do good and doeth it not, to him it is sin.") Also the legend of Christ and the man working on the Sabbath, to whom he said, "If thou knowest what thou doest, blessed art thou! But if thou knowest not what thou doest, cursed art thou!" If we are conscious, morality no longer exists. If we are not conscious, we are still slaves, and we are accursed if we obey not the law. He said that if we belong to the secret church, then we belong, and we need not worry about it, but can go our own way. If we do not belong, no amount of teaching or organization can bring us there.

Then I asked him about a single animus figure, and he said, "Many souls are young; they are promiscuous; they are prostitutes in the unconscious and sell themselves cheaply. They are like flowers that bloom and die and come again. Other souls are older, like trees or palms. They find, or must seek, one complete animus, who shall perhaps be many in one. And when they find him, it is like the closing of an electric circuit. Then they know the meaning of life.

"But to have an animus like an archimandrite[2] is as if to say, You are a priest of the Mysteries. And this needs a great humility to counterbalance it. You need to go down to the level of the mice. And as a tree, so great as the height of its branches, so deep must be the depths of its roots. And the meaning of the tree is neither in the roots, nor in the uplifted crown, but in the life in between them."

Then I asked him how to get the mean between the two worlds, between the world of the unconscious and that of reality. He replied, "You are the mediator. It is in your immediate life that they meet. In the pleroma they are merged—in nature they are one—and the primitive is always striving up against its oneness. The glacier is always there. Our civilization finds an adaptation that will satisfy these things for a while, and they are quiet. Then they begin to come up again, and again we find a new adaptation, and they are quiet once more. Today we are in a period of great transition, and they come up again. Eventually they will swallow man, but it will not be the same again, for he has attained the union of the opposites through their separation. Possibly, after man will come a period of the animal and then again the plant—who knows?—and who or what will carry on the lamp of consciousness? Who knows?"

[2] Dr. Harding had dreamed of an abbot, an archimandrite.—E.F.E.

VI. THE ANIMA

CONCERNING THE ARCHETYPES WITH SPECIAL REFERENCE TO THE ANIMA CONCEPT

134 These few examples may suffice to characterize the experience of projection and those features of it which are independent of tradition. We can hardly get round the hypothesis that an emotionally charged content is lying ready in the unconscious and springs into projection at a certain moment. This content is the syzygy motif, and it expresses the fact that a masculine element is always paired with a feminine one. The wide distribution and extraordinary emotionality of this motif prove that it is a fundamental psychic factor of great practical importance, no matter whether the individual psychotherapist or psychologist understands where and in what way it influences his special field of work. Microbes, as we know, played their dangerous role long before they were discovered.

135 As I have said, it is natural to suspect the parental pair in all syzygies. The feminine part, the mother, corresponds to the anima. But since, for the reasons discussed above, consciousness of the object prevents its projection, there is nothing for it but to assume that parents are also the least known of all human beings, and consequently that an unconscious reflection of the parental pair exists which is as unlike them, as utterly alien and incommensurable, as a man compared with a god. It would be conceivable, and has as we know been asserted, that the unconscious reflection is none other than the image of father and mother that was acquired in early childhood, overvalued, and later repressed on account of the incest-fantasy associated with it. This hypothesis presupposes that the image was once *conscious,* otherwise it could not have been "repressed." It also presupposes that the act of moral repression has itself become unconscious, for otherwise the act would remain preserved in

consciousness together with the memory of the repressive moral reaction, from which the nature of the thing repressed could easily be recognized. I do not want to enlarge on these misgivings, but would merely like to emphasize that there is general agreement on one point: that the parental imago comes into existence not in the pre-puberal period or at a time when consciousness is more or less developed, but in the initial stages between the first and fourth year, when consciousness does not show any real continuity and is characterized by a kind of island-like discontinuity. The ego-relationship that is required for continuity of consciousness is present only in part, so that a large proportion of psychic life at this stage runs on in a state which can only be described as relatively unconscious. At all events it is a state which would give the impression of a somnambulistic, dream, or twilight state if observed in an adult. These states, as we know from the observation of small children, are always characterized by an apperception of reality filled with fantasies. The fantasy-images outweigh the influence of sensory stimuli and mould them into conformity with a *pre-existing psychic image*.

¹³⁶ It is in my view a great mistake to suppose that the psyche of a new-born child is a *tabula rasa* in the sense that there is absolutely nothing in it. In so far as the child is born with a differentiated brain that is predetermined by heredity and therefore individualized, it meets sensory stimuli coming from outside not with *any* aptitudes, but with *specific* ones, and this necessarily results in a particular, individual choice and pattern of apperception. These aptitudes can be shown to be inherited instincts and preformed patterns, the latter being the *a priori* and formal conditions of apperception that are based on instinct. Their presence gives the world of the child and the dreamer its anthropomorphic stamp. They are the archetypes, which direct all fantasy activity into its appointed paths and in this way produce, in the fantasy-images of children's dreams as well as in the delusions of schizophrenia, astonishing mythological parallels such as can also be found, though in lesser degree, in the dreams of normal persons and neurotics. It is not, therefore, a question of inherited *ideas* but of inherited *possibilities* of ideas. Nor are they individual acquisitions but, in the main,

common to all, as can be seen from the universal occurrence of the archetypes.[25]

137   Just as the archetypes occur on the ethnological level as myths, so also they are found in every individual, and their effect is always strongest, that is, they anthropomorphize reality most, where consciousness is weakest and most restricted, and where fantasy can overrun the facts of the outer world. This condition is undoubtedly present in the child during the first years of its life. It therefore seems to me more probable that the archetypal form of the divine syzygy first covers up and assimilates the image of the real parents until, with increasing consciousness, the real figures of the parents are perceived— often to the child's disappointment. Nobody knows better than the psychotherapist that the mythologizing of the parents is often pursued far into adulthood and is given up only with the greatest resistance.

138   I remember a case that was presented to me as the victim of a high-grade mother and castration complex, which had still not been overcome in spite of psychoanalysis. Without any hint from me, the man had made some drawings which showed the mother first as a superhuman being, and then as a figure of woe, with bloody mutilations. I was especially struck by the fact that a castration had obviously been performed on the mother, for in front of her gory genitals lay the cut-off male sexual organs. The drawings clearly represented a diminishing climax: first the mother was a divine hermaphrodite, who then, through the son's disappointing experience of reality, was robbed of its androgynous, Platonic perfection and changed into the woeful figure of an ordinary old woman. Thus from the very beginning, from the son's earliest childhood, the mother was assimilated to the archetypal idea of the syzygy, or conjunction of male and female, and for this reason appeared perfect and super-

25 Hubert and Mauss (*Mélanges d'histoire des religions*, preface, p. xxix) call these *a priori* thought-forms "categories," presumably with reference to Kant: "They exist ordinarily as habits which govern consciousness, but are themselves unconscious." The authors conjecture that the primordial images are conditioned by language. This conjecture may be correct in certain cases, but in general it is contradicted by the fact that a great many archetypal images and associations are brought to light by dream psychology and psychopathology which would be absolutely incommunicable through language.

human.[26] The latter quality invariably attaches to the archetype and explains why the archetype appears strange and as if not belonging to consciousness, and also why, if the subject identifies with it, it often causes a devastating change of personality, generally in the form of megalomania or its opposite.

139   The son's disappointment effected a castration of the hermaphroditic mother: this was the patient's so-called castration complex. He had tumbled down from his childhood Olympus and was no longer the son-hero of a divine mother. His so-called fear of castration was fear of real life, which refused to come up to his erstwhile childish expectations, and everywhere lacked that mythological meaning which he still dimly remembered from his earliest youth. His life was, in the truest sense of the word, "godless." And that, for him—though he did not realize it—meant a dire loss of hope and energy. He thought of himself as "castrated," which is a very plausible neurotic misunderstanding—so plausible that it could even be turned into a theory of neurosis.

140   Because people have always feared that the connection with the instinctive, archetypal stage of consciousness might get lost in the course of life, the custom has long since been adopted of giving the new-born child, in addition to his bodily parents, two godparents, a "godfather" and a "godmother," who are supposed to be responsible for the spiritual welfare of their godchild. They represent the pair of gods who appear at its birth, thus illustrating the "dual birth" motif.[27]

26 Conforming to the bisexual Original Man in Plato, *Symposium,* XIV, and to the hermaphroditic Primal Beings in general.
27 The "dual birth" refers to the motif, well known from hero mythology, which makes the hero descend from divine as well as from human parents. In most mysteries and religions it plays an important role as a baptism or rebirth motif. It was this motif that misled Freud in his study of Leonardo da Vinci. Without taking account of the fact that Leonardo was by no means the only artist to paint the motif of St. Anne, Mary, and the Christ-child, Freud tried to reduce Anne and Mary, the grandmother and mother, to the mother and stepmother of Leonardo; in other words, to assimilate the painting to his theory. But did the other painters all have stepmothers?! What prompted Freud to this violent interpretation was obviously the fantasy of dual descent suggested by Leonardo's biography. This fantasy covered up the inconvenient reality that St. Anne was the grandmother, and prevented Freud from inquiring into the biographies of other artists who also painted St. Anne. The "religious inhibition of thought" mentioned on p. 79 (1957 edn.) proved true of the author himself. Similarly, the incest theory on

141   The anima image, which lends the mother such superhuman glamour in the eyes of the son, gradually becomes tarnished by commonplace reality and sinks back into the unconscious, but without in any way losing its original tension and instinctivity. It is ready to spring out and project itself at the first opportunity, the moment a woman makes an impression that is out of the ordinary. We then have Goethe's experience with Frau von Stein, and its repercussions in the figures of Mignon and Gretchen, all over again. In the case of Gretchen, Goethe also showed us the whole underlying "metaphysic." The love life of a man reveals the psychology of this archetype in the form either of boundless fascination, overvaluation, and infatuation, or of misogyny in all its gradations and variants, none of which can be explained by the real nature of the "object" in question, but only by a transference of the mother complex. The complex, however, was caused in the first place by the assimilation of the mother (in itself a normal and ubiquitous phenomenon) to the pre-existent, feminine side of an archetypal "male-female" pair of opposites, and secondly by an abnormal delay in detaching from the primordial image of the mother. Actually, nobody can stand the total loss of the archetype. When that happens, it gives rise to that frightful "discontent in our culture," where nobody feels at home because a "father" and "mother" are missing. Everyone knows the provisions that religion has always made in this respect. Unfortunately there are very many people who thoughtlessly go on asking whether these provisions are "true," when it is really a question of a psychological need. Nothing is achieved by explaining them away rationalistically.

142   When projected, the anima always has a feminine form with definite characteristics. This empirical finding does not mean

which he lays so much stress is based on another archetype, the well-known incest motif frequently met with in hero myths. It is logically derived from the original hermaphrodite type, which seems to go far back into prehistory. Whenever a psychological theory is forcibly applied, we have reason to suspect that an archetypal fantasy-image is trying to distort reality, thus bearing out Freud's own idea of the "religious inhibition of thought." But to explain the genesis of archetypes by means of the incest theory is about as useful as ladling water from one kettle into another kettle standing beside it, which is connected with the first by a pipe. You cannot explain one archetype by another; that is, it is impossible to say where the archetype comes from, because there is no Archimedean point outside the *a priori* conditions it represents.

that the archetype is constituted like that *in itself.* The male-female syzygy is only one among the possible pairs of opposites, albeit the most important one in practice and the commonest. It has numerous connections with other pairs which do not display any sex differences at all and can therefore be put into the sexual category only by main force. These connections, with their manifold shades of meaning, are found more particularly in Kundalini yoga,[28] in Gnosticism,[29] and above all in alchemical philosophy,[30] quite apart from the spontaneous fantasy-products in neurotic and psychotic case material. When one carefully considers this accumulation of data, it begins to seem probable that an archetype in its quiescent, unprojected state has no exactly determinable form but is in itself an indefinite structure which can assume definite forms only in projection.

143   This seems to contradict the concept of a "type." If I am not mistaken, it not only seems but actually *is* a contradiction. Empirically speaking, we are dealing all the time with "types," definite forms that can be named and distinguished. But as soon as you divest these types of the phenomenology presented by the case material, and try to examine them in relation to other archetypal forms, they branch out into such far-reaching ramifications in the history of symbols that one comes to the conclusion that the basic psychic elements are infinitely varied and ever changing, so as utterly to defy our powers of imagination. The empiricist must therefore content himself with a theoretical "as if." In this respect he is no worse off than the atomic physicist, even though his method is not based on quantitative measurement but is a morphologically descriptive one.

144   The anima is a factor of the utmost importance in the psychology of a man wherever emotions and affects are at work. She intensifies, exaggerates, falsifies, and mythologizes all emotional relations with his work and with other people of both sexes. The resultant fantasies and entanglements are all her doing. When the anima is strongly constellated, she softens the man's character and makes him touchy, irritable, moody, jealous, vain, and unadjusted. He is then in a state of "discontent" and spreads

---

28 Cf. Avalon, *The Serpent Power; Shri-Chakra-Sambhara Tantra;* Woodroffe, *Shakti and Shakta.*
29 Schultz, *Dokumente der Gnosis,* especially the lists in Irenaeus, *Adversus haereses.*   30 Cf. *Psychology and Alchemy.*

discontent all around him. Sometimes the man's relationship to the woman who has caught his anima accounts for the existence of this syndrome.

145 The anima, as I have remarked elsewhere,[31] has not escaped the attentions of the poets. There are excellent descriptions of her, which at the same time tell us about the symbolic context in which the archetype is usually embedded. I give first place to Rider Haggard's novels *She, The Return of She,* and *Wisdom's Daughter,* and Benoît's *L'Atlantide.* Benoît was accused of plagiarizing Rider Haggard, because the two accounts are disconcertingly alike. But it seems he was able to acquit himself of this charge. Spitteler's *Prometheus* contains some very subtle observations, too, and his novel *Imago* gives an admirable description of projection.

146 The question of *therapy* is a problem that cannot be disposed of in a few words. It was not my intention to deal with it here, but I would like to outline my point of view. Younger people, who have not yet reached the middle of life (around the age of 35), can bear even the total loss of the anima without injury. The important thing at this stage is for a man to be a man. The growing youth must be able to free himself from the anima fascination of his mother. There are exceptions, notably artists, where the problem often takes a different turn; also homosexuality, which is usually characterized by identity with the anima. In view of the recognized frequency of this phenomenon, its interpretation as a pathological perversion is very dubious. The psychological findings show that it is rather a matter of incomplete detachment from the hermaphroditic archetype, coupled with a distinct resistance to identify with the role of a one-sided sexual being. Such a disposition should not be adjudged negative in all circumstances, in so far as it preserves the archetype of the Original Man, which a one-sided sexual being has, up to a point, lost.

147 After the middle of life, however, permanent loss of the anima means a diminution of vitality, of flexibility, and of human kindness. The result, as a rule, is premature rigidity, crustiness, stereotypy, fanatical one-sidedness, obstinacy, pedantry, or else resignation, weariness, sloppiness, irresponsibility, and finally a childish *ramollissement* with a tendency to alcohol. After

31 Cf. the first paper in this volume.

middle life, therefore, the connection with the archetypal sphere of experience should if possible be re-established.[32]

[32] The most important problems for therapy are discussed in my essay "The Relations between the Ego and the Unconscious" and also in the "Psychology of the Transference." For the mythological aspects of the anima, the reader is referred to another paper in this volume, "The Psychological Aspects of the Kore."

THE PERSONIFICATION OF THE OPPOSITES
INTERPRETATION AND MEANING OF SALT

Jung's alchemical writings are exercises in hermeneutics, interpretations grounded in his intuition that in their philosophic treatises on the nature of chemical materials, the alchemists projected psychological processes onto matter. Much of the unconscious masculine nature was the substance sulphur, which contributed to the fiery character of Sol. But in the formation of the man's lunar unconscious, which had a feminine character, the root substance appeared to be salt, associated throughout human history with tears. Jung's understanding of the importance of experiences of bitter disappointment in the development of the anima reaches beyond the traditional Christian emphasis on suffering and sacrifice embodied in the Virgin Mary to the more seasoned femininity of the Gnostic Sophia, who personifies earth wisdom.

---

330   Apart from its lunar wetness and its terrestrial nature, the most outstanding properties of salt are bitterness and wisdom. As in the double quaternio of the elements and qualities, earth and water have coldness in common, so bitterness and wisdom would form a pair of opposites with a third thing between. (See diagram on facing page.) The factor common to both, however incommensurable the two ideas may seem, is, psychologically, the function of *feeling*. Tears, sorrow, and disappointment are bitter, but wisdom is the comforter in all psychic suffering. Indeed, bitterness and wisdom form a pair of alternatives: where there is bitterness wisdom is lacking, and where wisdom is there can be no bitterness. Salt, as the carrier of this fateful alternative,

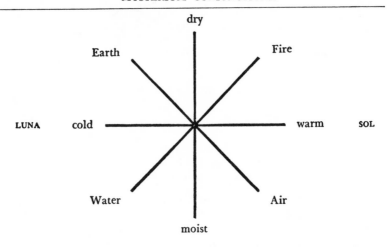

is co-ordinated with the nature of woman. The masculine, solar nature in the right half of the quaternio knows neither coldness, nor a shadow, nor heaviness, melancholy, etc., because, so long as all goes well, it identifies as closely as possible with consciousness, and that as a rule is the idea which one has of oneself. In this idea the shadow is usually missing: first because nobody likes to admit to any inferiority, and second because logic forbids something white to be called black. A good man has good qualities, and only the bad man has bad qualities. For reasons of prestige we pass over the shadow in complete silence. A famous example of masculine prejudice is Nietzsche's Superman, who scorns compassion and fights against the "Ugliest Man"—the ordinary man that everyone is. The shadow must not be seen, it must be denied, repressed, or twisted into something quite extraordinary. The sun is always shining and everything smiles back. There is no room for any prestige-diminishing weakness, so the *sol niger* is never seen. Only in solitary hours is its presence feared.

331   Things are different with Luna: every month she is darkened and extinguished; she cannot hide this from anybody, not even from herself. She knows that this same Luna is now bright and now dark—but who has ever heard of a dark sun? We call this quality of Luna "woman's closeness to nature," and the fiery brilliance and hot air that plays round the surface of things we like to call "the masculine mind."

332   Despite all attempts at denial and obfuscation there is an

124

unconscious factor, a black sun, which is responsible for the surprisingly common phenomenon of masculine split-mindedness, when the right hand mustn't know what the left is doing. This split in the masculine psyche and the regular darkening of the moon in woman together explain the remarkable fact that the woman is accused of all the darkness in a man, while he himself basks in the thought that he is a veritable fount of vitality and illumination for all the females in his environment. Actually, he would be better advised to shroud the brilliance of his mind in the profoundest doubt. It is not difficult for this type of mind (which besides other things is a great trickster like Mercurius) to admit a host of sins in the most convincing way, and even to combine it with a spurious feeling of ethical superiority without in the least approximating to a genuine insight. This can never be achieved without the participation of feeling; but the intellect admits feeling only when it is convenient. The novilunium of woman is a source of countless disappointments for man which easily turn to bitterness, though they could equally well be a source of wisdom if they were understood. Naturally this is possible only if he is prepared to acknowledge his black sun, that is, his shadow.

333   Confirmation of our interpretation of salt as Eros (i.e., as a feeling relationship) is found in the fact that the bitterness is the origin of the *colours* (par. 245). We have only to look at the drawings and paintings of patients who supplement their analysis by active imagination to see that colours are feeling-values. Mostly, to begin with, only a pencil or pen is used to make rapid sketches of dreams, sudden ideas, and fantasies. But from a certain moment on the patients begin to make use of colour, and this is generally the moment when merely intellectual interest gives way to emotional participation. Occasionally the same phenomenon can be observed in dreams, which at such moments are dreamt in colour, or a particularly vivid colour is insisted upon.

To Jolande Jacobi

Dear Dr. Jacobi,   Bollingen, 26 August 1943

. . .

   The mistake you are making consists in your being drawn too much into X.'s neurotic problem. This is evident from the fact, for instance, that your animus is trying like mad to interpret when there is nothing to be interpreted. *Why* does he say he has other relationships? Why indeed! As though anyone knew. He just says it. That is very nice of him, inconsiderate, truthful, tactless, unpremeditated, confiding, etc., etc. If you knew the *real* reason you would also know who X. was at his birth and at his death. But we shall only find that out in the Hereafter. He has absolutely no reason he can state, it has simply happened and can be interpreted quite superflously in a hundred different ways, and no single interpretation holds water, being merely an insistence which, once made, only has the effect of driving him into further whimsical and uninterpretable reactions. In reality his irrational behaviour represents the conscious and unconscious sides of the anima, and is absolutely necessary in order to gain insight into her, just as in general he needs a bevy of women in order to grasp the essence of this glamorous figure. Of course he is still too naïve to notice this. But you, just as naïvely, have intruded yourself as an anima figure into this witches' sabbath and are therefore caught up in the dance as though you were nothing but an anima. Wherever you stick a finger in out of "love" or involuntary participation you will burn it, for it is not involvement that is expected of you, but objective, disincarnate observation, and if you want to snatch something out of it for the heart—and no reasonable objection can be made to this—you must pay for it in blood, as was always so and always will be. At least one must keep one's head out of it so as not to be eaten up entirely by emotional ape-men. Where there are emotional ties one is always the disappointed disappointer. This one has to know if one wants, or is forced, to participate correctly.

. . .

   With cordial greetings,

                            Yours sincerely, C . G . JUNG

126

LECTURE V

19 February 1930

Dr. Jung:

I have brought you today the picture[1] of which I spoke last week, the reproduction of the Tibetan mandala. It is a *yantra*, used for the purpose of concentration upon the most philosophical thought of the Tibetan Lamas. It shows in the innermost circle the diamond wedge or thunderbolt, that symbol of potential energy, and the white light symbolizing absolute truth. And here are the four functions, the four fields of colour, and then the four gates to the world. Then comes the gazelle garden, and finally the ring of the fire of desirousness outside. You will notice that it is embedded in the earth region exactly to the middle, with the upper part reaching to the celestial world. The figures above are three great teachers, the living Buddhas or Bodhisattvas, two yellow and one red. That has to do with the Tibetan Lamaistic doctrine. They correspond to the mountains on the earth below. What the mountain is on earth the great teacher is among men. I have another mandala where, instead of a thunderbolt in the centre, there is the god Mahasukha, one form of the Indian god Shiva, in the embrace of his wife Shakti. Today I think we will continue our dreams.

Dream [23]

Our patient says that he is at a sort of festival celebration in a Protestant church, in which the benches are not all arranged in the

---

[1] Jung published the yantra as a frontispiece to *The Secret of the Golden Flower* (in orig., 1929, and tr., 1931) and again in *Psychology and Alchemy* (1944), CW 12, fig. 43 (described there as a Tibetan painted banner, formerly in the China Institute, Frankfurt, and destroyed in World War II). He published it again with "Concerning Mandala Symbolism" (1950), CW 9 i, fig. 1, analyzed in pars. 630-38.

same direction but in the form of a square, so that they all face the pulpit, which is in the middle of one of the long walls of the church. A hymn is being sung, a very well-known one, typical of our Christmas festivals: "O du fröhliche, O du selige Weihnachtszeit."[2] (One hears it everywhere at that time of the year.) He joins in the singing of the hymn and suddenly hears somebody behind him singing the same words in a peculiar soprano voice, exceedingly loud and the melody quite different, so that everyone around that person gets completely out of tune. Our dreamer immediately stops and looks back to see who the singer can be. It is a man sitting on a bench at right angles to his own and wearing, strangely enough, a sort of woman's garment, so that he feels unable to make out positively whether it is a man or a woman. Then the service comes to an end, and on going out, he finds he has left his hat and overcoat in the wardrobe. (He was thinking naturally not of the word "wardrobe," but of "garde-robe" which is of course really a French word, but in French one would say "vestiaire". "Garde-robe" is used in German, taken over from the old French word, which originally meant the man who takes care of the wraps.) On the way back to the wardrobe, he wonders whether the word "garde-robe" in French is a masculine or feminine noun, and he comes to the conclusion that one should say "le garde-robe," and not, as it is used in German as a feminine noun, "die Garde-robe." While thinking of that, he suddenly hears the singer talking to a man who is with him, saying that today he has shown for once that he too can sing. Our dreamer again turns back to look at him and has to restrain himself from making a disagreeable remark to him. He notices that he appears more masculine this time and that he has a Jewish type of face, and then seems to know who he is and remembers that his son is a friend of his. Then the son suddenly appears and violently reproaches his father because he upset the hymn.

Associations: As a child he had been *forced to go to church* every Sunday. On account of that compulsion, he developed an antipathy to churches and parsons, which is the reason that he almost never goes to church except on special festivals. The church in which the benches are arranged as he described, all facing the pulpit, is the church to which he had been made to go as a boy.

[2] Sung to the tune "Sanctissima," usually with the English words "O thou joyful day, O thou blessed day, Holy, peaceful Christmastide."

Concerning the *hymn* he says, "When I think of that hymn, I think of the end, the refrain, 'Freue dich O Christenheit,' meaning 'Rejoice, O Christendom.' "

Then he associates with his joining in the hymn the fact that he *cannot sing*. He is quite unmusical, and if he tried he would probably upset the melody as much as the man who sang an entirely different melody in a high woman's soprano.

With the peculiar *singer, whose sex is uncertain*, he associates the fact that he, as a boy, read a book called *Der Golem* by Meyrink.[3] (That is quite a remarkable book; I think it has now been translated into English.) You remember that in a former seminar he dreamed of a square building where he climbed over a fence. We spoke especially of his associations with the end of that book, *Der Golem*, where the hero comes to the locked gates. Here again he associates just that last scene, where the hero arrives at the supreme moment when he really should find the answer to all riddles, the supreme solution of the whole problem, but then comes to the locked gate upon which is the symbol of the hermaphrodite. The dreamer says that this symbol of the hermaphrodite means, as he would interpret it, the alchemical nuptial, that is, the blending of the male and female in one indivisible whole. He says that he can't help feeling that that song would sound very different from the hymn in the Protestant church—in other words, that such ideas would not fit in with the ideas of the Protestant church and would prove most disturbing. Obviously!

Concerning the word "garde-robe," the uncertainty whether it is masculine or feminine refers naturally to the same thing as the dubious sex of the man, and again he associates the hermaphrodite symbol.

As to the discovery that the *singer is Jewish*, he says that he thinks Meyrink must be a Jew; he is convinced that even if he does not confess to it, his creed would be Judaic, he would be reserving in the secret room of his soul the Judaic conviction. That would explain, he says, why Meyrink in his book *The Green Face*[4] sends the hero to Brazil to save him when the continent of Europe collapses. You see, that book has a somewhat unsatisfactory ending. Apparently Meyrink got very involved in a complicated plot and did not

---

[3] See above, 19 June 1929, n. 6, and text following.
[4] Gustav Meyrink, *Das grüne Gesicht* (Leipzig, 1916).

know how to find his way out of the tangle; then by divine providence, a great storm came up and devastated the whole Occident and got him out of the difficulty of a satisfactory solution. His hero, Sephardi, the Jewish scholar, having foreseen it, had collected his family and friends and emigrated to Brazil unharmed, as it is a local storm in Europe only. Obviously the dreamer means that Meyrink, being a Jew, saves his tribesmen in the fatal moment and nobody else, a sort of exodus out of the cursed land.

You probably would not have expected such a dream after the ones before, I certainly would not have guessed it. That is the wonderful irrationality of the unconscious which always beats us. I would not have foreseen it—except in one respect: that last mandala dream would upset certain Occidental convictions, and as this man has had a definite religious education of a narrow kind, he cannot help preserving certain prejudices which would be cruelly hurt by the ideas of the mandala psychology, because that brings a new ethical orientation. It is a point of view that does not fit into the Christian standpoint, which divides the world into good and evil and does not allow any reconciliation. The whole of Christian eschatology follows this line of thought in teaching about the ultimate things—that at the end of the world there will be a Last Judgment where good and evil are divided definitely and forever by those two remarkable institutions Heaven and Hell. All the evil ones will be cast into hell and will cook there forever, and the good ones will attain that blissful condition where they are allowed to make music during all eternity. This is a dogmatic statement of the irreconcilability of good and evil. Nothing to be done about it, just give up, no choice. But the mandala psychology is of a very different kind: an endless chain of lives moving on through good and evil, through all aspects of things. The eternally revolving wheel of existence, now in the shadow, now in the light. This is an extraordinary relativation of the ethical problem—that having been high you will be low, having been low you will be high. Out of the darkness comes the light, and after the light comes again the darkness, so evil is not so bad and good is not so good because they are related and only together by a mistake which remains inexplicable. Why, after all, is it not perfect since it is the work of a perfect Master? The Occidental answer is: because the devil put some dirt into it, or man was such an ass that he spoiled it somehow, this work of an omnipotent and omniscient Being. The fact of evil was the cause of the invention of the devil, who double-crossed the good intentions of the perfect Master.

In the Eastern mandala psychology, all this takes on an entirely different aspect. Relativity is rather shocking to a Westerner. It intimates a certain indulgence even, and to a puritanical mind that is almost unbearable. That is the case with this man. It would not be so much so in theory. He does not go to church, he does not follow the traditional creed; but when it comes to practical life it is a bit awkward, because our church views are all linked up with our real god, which is respectability, the eyes of the community. When he comes to that, the real god, and his fear of those eyes, he collapses into a terrible conflict.

Now, if he has really understood the meaning of the last dream, that the machine is now going to function, it would indicate that he is about to enter life in a new way, where every wheel is in place and where the machine will yield the all-around life which it is meant to yield, a complete life, with light and shadow. But no sooner is he at that point than he hurts himself against traditional convictions, and this next dream contains obviously the problem of the offended Western values. Therefore he is brought instantly back to his childhood, when he was forced to go to church. It is as if a voice from within said, "Remember the days when you were still in the church and believed these things. How can you get away from that? You are still there singing the same song as the whole Christian community." And then comes the first disturbance, that soprano voice. Now where does that soprano voice come from?

Miss Howells: It is the feminine side of himself, the anima.

Dr. Jung: Sure! It is Madame Anima who suddenly begins to sing too. He was singing the song of the community as if he were a perfectly respectable member of that church, and then the anima breaks in with an entirely unsuitable song. And what does that melody express? Not the words, but the melody. What is the value of that?

Answer: Feeling.

Dr. Jung: Yes, nothing is more impressive than an organ. When you are reminded of a Protestant church you just yawn, a terrible bore, but when you hear the music, you cannot help having feeling, it stirs you. Perhaps not if you go regularly, but a man like myself, who has not been to church for an eternity, will naturally have a sentimental feeling—a beautiful remembrance which appeals to one's feeling. It is wrong not to acknowledge it. A sermon is tedious, while music pulls at the heart. So it is very typical that the dream speaks of feelings, which are really dangerous in a man's case. In his thinking these ideas have no hold on him any longer; he is firm in his convictions. But the music gets him, and he is ground under. He is drawn in and cannot help singing, so he gets into a situation or mood that is quite opposed to the intention mentioned in the dream before. Then the conflict arises in his feeling sphere, and that is why his anima begins to sing. The anima is always connected with the inferior function. As he is an intellectual, his feelings are somewhat inferior, and she is like a personification of his inferior feeling function. Why does the anima not sing the church song? Why an entirely different melody?

Mrs. Baynes: To tell him she is there.

Dr. Jung: But what for?

Mrs. Baynes: Because she wants to make trouble.

Dr. Jung: That would be almost a depreciation of the anima.

Mrs. Baynes: He does not appreciate her, so she wants to make herself felt.

Dr. Jung: But if she only wants to make herself felt or to make trouble, she could just as well be a dog that barks, or an automobile that begins whooping outside the church.

Mrs. Sigg: The anima has a different taste. It is not the taste of the Church, it would perhaps be more like the Indian style.

Dr. Jung: You mean more in favour of the mandala psychology? That is exceedingly probable, because the anima has to be excluded from the Christian frame. She is eternally a heretic and does not fit in at all, a perfect pagan, in more or less open revolt against the Christian point of view. Perhaps you are astonished that I speak of her in such a personal way, but that has forever been the way of taking her, that figure has always been expressed by poets in a personal form. Usually she is projected into a real woman, who thereby becomes more imaginary, like the Lady of the Troubadours and the Knights of the Cours d'Amour,[5] slightly divine. Then you know how Rider Haggard speaks of "She who must be obeyed";[6] he makes her a very definite figure. So to give her the right quality we must describe her as a personality and not as a scientific ab-

[5] These concepts belong to the chivalric tradition of medieval Western Europe.
[6] See above, 12 Dec. 1928, n. 8.

straction. In zoology you can speak of the species, the *whale*. But there are many different kinds of whales, you must say *which* whale, and then it has a specific value. The anima represents the primitive layer of man's psychology, and primitive psychology shuns abstractions. There are practically no concepts in primitive languages. In Arabic, there are sixty words for types of camel and no word for camel in the abstract. Ask an Arab the word for camel and he does not know. It is either an old, or a young, or a female camel, etc., each called by a different name. In a language more primitive still there are thirty different words for cutting—cutting with a knife, a sword, string, etc.—and no word for the act of cutting.

My particular friend Steiner[7] supposes that there were pre-stages of the earth, one a globe of fire, another a globe of gases, and on one of them, he says, there could even be observed some sensations of taste. Now, whose were the sensations of taste? There is no such thing as abstract sensation, some sensation suspended in space to the Big Dipper or Sirius. In one Negro language there are fifty expressions for walking, but not one for the act of walking; one cannot say, "I am walking." Nor is there a word for *man*. We have all these abstract concepts, and in a way they are misleading, or rather, not informing. We can say a man or a woman or, even more indefinite, a person wants to speak to you, and how little we know—whether he or she is outside, inside, standing up, alive or dead. A primitive telling you the same thing by the very nature of his language would inform you, for instance, that an alive, erect man was standing outside your door. There are no words in their language for a man without an almost complete description. They have the most curious expressions for walking which describe exactly how it is done, each specific case of walking, with knees bent, on his heels, etc., so if you hear of him at all you can fairly see that man moving. It is an almost grotesque description of each subject. This absence of collective notions is absolutely characteristic of the primitive mind.

Now, concerning my concept of the anima, I have been reproached occasionally by scholars for using an almost mythological term to express a scientific fact. They expect me to translate her

---

[7] Rudolf Steiner (1861-1925), German occultist, first a Theosophist, then the founder of Anthroposophy, an offshoot of Theosophy. The reference here is perhaps to his book *Wie erlangt man Erkenntnisse der höheren Welten?* (1922) (= "How does one attain knowledge of higher worlds?"), a copy of which Jung owned.

into scientific terminology, which would deprive the figure of its—or her—specific life. If you say, for instance, that the anima is a function of connection or relationship between the conscious and unconscious, that is a very pale thing. It is as if you should show a picture of a great philosopher and call it simply *Homo sapiens*; of course a picture of a criminal or an idiot would be *Homo sapiens* just as well. The scientific term conveys nothing, and the merely abstract notion of the anima conveys nothing, but when you say the anima is almost personal, a complex that behaves exactly as if she were a little person, or at times as if she were a very important person, then you get it about right. Therefore, chiefly for practical purposes, I leave the anima in her personified form, just as I would in describing President Wilson, or Bismarck, or Mussolini. I would not say they were specimens of *Homo sapiens*, I deal with them specifically as they are. And so the anima is personal and specific. Otherwise it is just a function, as intuition or thinking are functions. But that does not cover the actual facts, nor does it express the extraordinary personality of the anima, the absolutely recognizable personality, so that one can easily point it out anywhere. Therefore I quite intentionally keep to the very personal term, meaning that she is a personal factor, almost as good as a person.

Naturally there is danger on the other side that people think she is a sort of ghost. Sure enough, to the primitive mind she is a ghost. She is a definite entity, and, if you are in a very primitive mood, you might see her in the form of a ghost—a smoke figure or a breath figure. She may become an hallucination. One sees that, for instance, in lunatics when they are possessed by the anima. Not very long ago I was called in as consulting physician to see an insane boy in a clinic in Zurich. When I came into the room he greeted me very politely and said, "You will probably not believe it, but I am my sister and I am a Buddhist." He has actually a married sister, but she plays no role in his life. He thought it was just a mistake that people took him for a man, and even declared that it was a malevolent invention on the part of his mother. To him that anima sister was absolutely real, more real than himself, he was identical with her. She was a Buddhist and therefore initiated into the mysteries of the East, and she had an Indian name, which was an extraordinarily clever contrivance. I don't remember it exactly, but it consisted of three syllables, and the middle syllable was *dava*, which is a Hindu word for divine. It was half Italian and half Hindu or Sanskrit and a bit of Greek. It was a typical designation, and the meaning was divine-mistress-sister. I have known many other cases where men have felt the anima as an extraordinary reality. I am quite certain that Rider Haggard could not possibly have written such an interminable series of novels if the anima had not been extremely real to him. That is the reason why I stress the personal character so much. We have to deal with the figure in a form that is entirely different from the usual because it designates a living factor, despite the fact that this factor, under certain conditions of development, may lose all that personal character and transform into a mere function. But that can only be the case when the conscious attitude is such that it loses the quality and characteristics of a human being—that is the mandala psychology.

Miss Howells: Is it common for her to take on the quality of the Orient or an older civilization? Here she is a Jewess.

Dr. Jung: It would seem so. In *She* the anima is an Oriental being, and in Pierre Bênoit's *Atlantide*.[8] The animus also. But we had better not talk of the animus now. It just scares me, it is much more difficult to deal with. The anima is definite and the animus is indefinite.

Question: Is the anima definitely a part of every man and every woman?

Dr. Jung: No, she is the female part of a man's psychology, so she would not naturally exist in a woman. When she does, she is absolutely identical with the woman's conscious principle, and then I would call it Eros. The same is true of a man reversed. Animus in a man is not a person, it is his conscious principle, and then I call it Logos.

In Chinese philosophy they speak of the masculine and feminine souls of a man. Therefore Wilhelm uses animus and anima exactly as I would. The terms animus and anima correspond to the Chinese *hun* and *kwei*,[9] but always they apply to a man. The Chinese were not concerned with women's psychology—as I unfortunately am! Even in the Middle Ages women were said to have no souls worth

---

[8] The novel *L'Atlantide* (1919), another work often cited by Jung, as early as March 1920; see letter quoted in *C. G. Jung: Word and Image* (1979), p. 151.

[9] In Wilhelm's discussion of the Chinese text (*Golden Flower*, 1962 edn., pp. 14f.) and in Jung's commentary (ibid., pp. 115ff.; CW 13, pars. 57-60), the Chinese word for anima is *p'o*; *kwei* is said to mean "demon" or "ghost of the departed one." Cary Baynes's footnote to Wilhelm (loc. cit.) aims to clarify the use of the terms.

mentioning, or only "little souls," like the story of the penguins in *L'île des pingouins*, by Anatole France.[10] Since St. Maël had baptized them, it became a question whether they had souls or not, and they at last called in St. Catherine of Alexandria to decide. "Well," she said, giving the final word in the celestial discussion, "Donnez-leur une âme immortelle, mais petite!" So in the Middle Ages women's psychology was *chose inconnue*, and similarly the old Chinese philosophers had the concept that the masculine animus was meant for heaven, while the female soul would become only a spectre, a phantom, who sinks into the earth after death. One goes on into Eternity and the other becomes a sort of haunting ghost, a demon. Therefore the Chinese meant by the animus in man what we mean by the Logos principle, or the conscious principle.

But since I have to deal with women's psychology as well as men's, I have found it better to call the conscious principle in man Logos, and the principle of relatedness in women Eros. The inferior Eros in man I designate as anima and the inferior Logos in woman as animus. These concepts, Logos and Eros, correspond roughly with the Christian idea of the soul. And the thing that does not fit in, the thing that sings the wrong tune, would be in a man the anima representing the Eros principle, and in a woman the animus representing the Logos principle, but in a sort of inferior form, a minor position. The reason why the anima is here playing that role of *diabolos in musica* is that the exclusive Logos principle in man does not allow for the Eros principle. He must discriminate, see things in their separateness, otherwise he is unable to recognize them. But that is against the principle of relatedness. A woman does not want to have things segregated, she wants to see them almost synchronized. A man who is possessed by his anima gets into the most awful difficulties, for he cannot discriminate, especially among women. While a woman under the law of the animus cannot relate, she becomes nothing but discrimination, surrounded by a wall of spiky cactus laws. She tells a man what he is up to and that chills him to the bone and he cannot get at her.

Now in regard to the particular role of the anima in this dream, that she is feminine is probably quite clear to you, but why is she masculine too? This is a very unusual case. And mind you, after-

---

[10] Jung relates the story in *Mysterium Coniunctionis* (1955), CW 14, par. 227, and briefly in his commentary on the *Tibetan Book of the Dead* (1935), CW 11, par. 835. Concerning Anatole France's novel *Penguin Island*, see above, 23 Jan. 1929, n. 2.

wards she becomes a man, a Jew. What do you think of the conditions under which a man's anima would be either male or hermaphroditic?

Answer: Homosexuality.

Dr. Jung: That is true. One often encounters anima figures of very doubtful sex, or quite indubitably masculine, when the conscious mind is feminine. But in the case of our dreamer there is no question of homosexuality. He is perhaps not quite free of perversions, everybody has the statistical amount; we all have that percentage of murder in our being, the whole population. But in him there is no trace of anything like repressed homosexuality. So why has he a masculine anima?

Mrs. Fierz: The anima is so incapable of making the man accept her that she has to play that role, use a sort of mimicry, to do so. It is the unconscious approaching the conscious.

Mrs. Sawyer: Isn't he identified with her and therefore she is masculine?

Dr. Jung: You mean since he cannot approach her he has to identify? Mrs. Fierz takes it from the unconscious side, that the unconscious is trying to make itself heard. Mrs. Sawyer sees it as the conscious trying to connect with the unconscious—his conscious possessed by the anima and so hermaphroditic. In either point of view one must detach her in order to establish a connection.

Mrs. Henley: Might it in this case simply express lack of development, because homosexuality is an attribute of youth?

Dr. Jung: That is also true, since he is undeveloped on the side of religion; from that point of view he could be expressed as a sort of homosexual boy about ten or twelve years old. That would be symbolic homosexuality. It is a fact that certain apparent sex perversions are merely symbolical; expressing an undeveloped state. In this case, there was no conscious manifestation of homosexuality that could be pointed out, so we may assume that this is symbolical homosexuality and not a disturbance of the normal. There have been traces of this feeling in some of his former dreams, in the dream of the Puer Aeternus, for instance, where he called the boy Eros and had a decided feeling of tenderness towards him.[11] And again in a dream which he had during our last seminar, that case

---

[11] Above, 13 Mar. 1929, p. 170.

of synchronicity, where he was worshipping the boy Telesphoros[12] and had doubts then also whether there was something homosexual about it. But it was merely symbolical, a certain immaturity, like the twelve-year-old condition. Such mental immaturity may be very local, it may refer to a specific expression of it, or it may go so far that a man is capable of believing that he actually is homosexual, in spite of the fact that he never had the experience. I have had men come to me complaining that they were homosexual, but when I say to such a man, "How was it? Did you get into trouble with boys," he exclaims indignantly that he would not touch a boy. "Men then?" "No." "Then why the devil do you call yourself homosexual?" And then he explains that a doctor said he was because he had had dreams where something homosexual happened. This simply means that the man in certain respects is not mature, and his immaturity may express itself in different ways—that he is not up to women, or not up to life, or not up to spiritual things. That must be the case here: that he is definitely immature in certain respects is expressed in the dream by his being brought back to his boyhood. Now in regard to what is he immature? Where is he unconscious?

Mrs. Deady: He can't manage his sexuality.

Dr. Jung: But you must keep in mind that he is a man who has allowed himself all sorts of things with fast women and who is not at all unaware of sexuality. His sex is wrong but not concretely. Now what is the trouble with him?

Dr. Deady: He has the sex of a boy of sixteen without feeling.

Dr. Jung: That is the point, no feeling. His sex is perfectly normal but it is unrelated sex, a sort of auto-eroticism, a kind of masturbation. There is no relation to the object, and that is probably the reason for the frigidity of his wife, and the reason of his other adventures. Eros is undeveloped, not his sexuality. That is by no means undeveloped, but his relationship to sexuality is wrong. In the last dream he was going to set his machine in motion, and the question came up whether the parts of the machine were properly related to the central part. All these functions, particularly his sexuality, have to be worked into the total mechanism. If unrelated, he naturally cannot function as a total personality. His sexuality must come into complete consideration, and he must have feelings

---

[12] Above, 11 Dec. 1929, p. 431.

about it. In other words, the Eros principle must be recognized. The reason why the anima appears is that she *is* Eros. And when he has the old point of view, singing the old song, Eros is repressed forever and the very devil. Therefore she comes up in church and disturbs the church hymn. His immaturity is expressed by the fact that he is back in his childhood and also by his symbolic homosexuality. If a man's anima is masculine, he is absolutely possessed—obsessed—by her, and he cannot establish a relationship with her until she is feminine. To say he is effeminate means the same thing—that she has power over him. The fact that the dream expresses is: you are effeminate, you are possessed by your anima.

VII. THE SPIRIT

THE PHENOMENOLOGY OF THE SPIRIT IN FAIRYTALES

The wise old man, subject of the excerpts that follow, is one of the easiest of all archetypes to recognize. In stories, he comes frequently to the aid of the *puer aeternus,* who derives support and counsel from his apparent maturity. When wisdom is a male rather than a female figure, a preexisting sagacity in the unconscious is indicated, rather than the archetypal wisdom that can only be won through bitter experience. Divinatory systems tap this faculty of omniscience in the psyche, which is an attribute of the archetypal Self. In every dream, this "wise" aspect of the self can be found, making its point about every life experience, assigning a meaning to it. This inner guide can be seductive. There is a tendency for the individual who comes in touch with this masculine source of wisdom to become isolated, identified, and inflated with him. Often this inflation leads to foolish and irresponsible acts. Jung's essay on Mercurius, some of which follows these excerpts, dissolves any simple notion of the unconscious as wise father by emphasizing the essential ambivalence of all psychic spirituality.

---

401   The frequency with which the spirit-type appears as an old man is about the same in fairytales as in dreams.[12] The old man always appears when the hero is in a hopeless and desperate situation from which only profound reflection or a lucky idea —in other words, a spiritual function or an endopsychic autom-

12 I am indebted to Mrs. H. von Roques and Dr. Marie-Louise von Franz for the fairytale material used here.

atism of some kind—can extricate him. But since, for internal and external reasons, the hero cannot accomplish this himself, the knowledge needed to compensate the deficiency comes in the form of a personified thought, i.e., in the shape of this sagacious and helpful old man. An Estonian fairytale,[13] for instance, tells how an ill-treated little orphan boy who had let a cow escape was afraid to return home again for fear of more punishment. So he ran away, chancing to luck. He naturally got himself into a hopeless situation, with no visible way out. Exhausted, he fell into a deep sleep. When he awoke, "it seemed to him that he had something liquid in his mouth, and he saw a little old man with a long grey beard standing before him, who was in the act of replacing the stopper in his little milk-flask. 'Give me some more to drink,' begged the boy. 'You have had enough for today,' replied the old man. 'If my path had not chanced to lead me to you, that would assuredly have been your last sleep, for when I found you, you were half dead.' Then the old man asked the boy who he was and where he wanted to go. The boy recounted everything he could remember happening to him up to the beating he had received the previous evening. 'My dear child,' said the old man, 'you are no better and no worse off than many others whose dear protectors and comforters rest in their coffins under the earth. You can no longer turn back. Now that you have run away, you must seek a new fortune in the world. As I have neither house nor home, nor wife nor child, I cannot take further care of you, but I will give you some good advice for nothing.' "

402   So far the old man has been expressing no more than what the boy, the hero of the tale, could have thought out for himself. Having given way to the stress of emotion and simply run off like that into the blue, he would at least have had to reflect that he needed food. It would also have been necessary, at such a moment, to consider his position. The whole story of his life up to the recent past would then have passed before his mind, as is usual in such cases. An anamnesis of this kind is a purpose-

---

13 *Finnische und estnische Volksmärchen*, No. 68, p. 208 ["How an Orphan Boy Unexpectedly Found His Luck"]. [All German collections of tales here cited are listed under "Folktales" in the bibliography, q.v. English titles of tales are given in brackets, though no attempt has been made to locate published translations. —EDITORS.]

ful process whose aim is to gather the assets of the whole personality together at the critical moment, when all one's spiritual and physical forces are challenged, and with this united strength to fling open the door of the future. No one can help the boy to do this; he has to rely entirely on himself. There is no going back. This realization will give the necessary resolution to his actions. By forcing him to face the issue, the old man saves him the trouble of making up his mind. Indeed the old man is himself this purposeful reflection and concentration of moral and physical forces that comes about spontaneously in the psychic space outside consciousness when conscious thought is not yet—or is no longer—possible. The concentration and tension of psychic forces have something about them that always looks like magic: they develop an unexpected power of endurance which is often superior to the conscious effort of will. One can observe this experimentally in the artificial concentration induced by hypnosis: in my demonstrations I used regularly to put an hysteric, of weak bodily build, into a deep hypnotic sleep and then get her to lie with the back of her head on one chair and her heels resting on another, stiff as a board, and leave her there for about a minute. Her pulse would gradually go up to 90. A husky young athlete among the students tried in vain to imitate this feat with a conscious effort of will. He collapsed in the middle with his pulse racing at 120.

403   When the clever old man had brought the boy to this point he could begin his good advice, i.e., the situation no longer looked hopeless. He advised him to continue his wanderings, always to the eastward, where after seven years he would reach the great mountain that betokened his good fortune. The bigness and tallness of the mountain are allusions to his adult personality.[14] Concentration of his powers brings assurance and is therefore the best guarantee of success.[15] From now on he will

---

14 The mountain stands for the goal of the pilgrimage and ascent, hence it often has the psychological meaning of the self. The *I Ching* describes the goal thus: "The king introduces him / To the Western Mountain" (Wilhelm/Baynes trans., 1967, p. 74—Hexagram 17, *Sui*, "Following"). Cf. Honorius of Autun (*Expositio in Cantica canticorum*, col. 389): "The mountains are prophets." Richard of St. Victor says: "Vis videre Christum transfiguratum? Ascende in montem istum, disce cognoscere te ipsum" (Do you wish to see the transfigured Christ? Ascend that mountain and learn to know yourself). (*Benjamin minor*, cols. 53–56.)

15 In this respect we would call attention to the phenomenology of yoga.

lack for nothing. "Take my scrip and my flask," says the old man, "and each day you will find in them all the food and drink you need." At the same time he gave him a burdock leaf that could change into a boat whenever the boy had to cross water.

404 Often the old man in fairytales asks questions like who? why? whence? and whither?[16] for the purpose of inducing self-reflection and mobilizing the moral forces, and more often still he gives the necessary magical talisman,[17] the unexpected and improbable power to succeed, which is one of the peculiarities of the unified personality in good or bad alike. But the intervention of the old man—the spontaneous objectivation of the archetype—would seem to be equally indispensable, since the conscious will by itself is hardly ever capable of uniting the personality to the point where it acquires this extraordinary power to succeed. For that, not only in fairytales but in life generally, the objective intervention of the archetype is needed, which checks the purely affective reactions with a chain of inner confrontations and realizations. These cause the who? where? how? why? to emerge clearly and in this wise bring knowledge of the immediate situation as well as of the goal. The resultant enlightenment and untying of the fatal tangle often has something positively magical about it—an experience not unknown to the psychotherapist.

405 The tendency of the old man to set one thinking also takes the form of urging people to "sleep on it." Thus he says to the girl who is searching for her lost brothers: "Lie down:

[16] There are numerous examples of this: *Spanische und Portugiesische Volksmärchen*, pp. 158, 199 ["The White Parrot" and "Queen Rose, or Little Tom"]; *Russische Volksmärchen*, p. 149 ["The Girl with No Hands"]; *Balkanmärchen*, p. 64 ["The Shepherd and the Three Samovilas (Nymphs)"]; *Märchen aus Iran*, pp. 150ff. ["The Secret of the Bath of Windburg"]; *Nordische Volksmärchen*, I, p. 231 ["The Werewolf"].

[17] To the girl looking for her brothers he gives a ball of thread that rolls towards them (*Finnische und Estnische Volksmärchen*, p. 260 ["The Contending Brothers"]). The prince who is searching for the kingdom of heaven is given a boat that goes by itself (*Deutsche Märchen seit Grimm*, pp. 381f. ["The Iron Boots"]). Other gifts are a flute that sets everybody dancing (*Balkanmärchen*, p. 173 ["The Twelve Crumbs"]), or the path-finding ball, the staff of invisibility (*Nordische Volksmärchen*, I, p. 97 ["The Princess with Twelve Pairs of Golden Shoes"]), miraculous dogs (ibid., p. 287 ["The Three Dogs"]), or a book of secret wisdom (*Chinesische Volksmärchen*, p. 258 ["Jang Liang"]).

morning is cleverer than evening." [18] He also sees through the gloomy situation of the hero who has got himself into trouble, or at least can give him such information as will help him on his journey. To this end he makes ready use of animals, particularly birds. To the prince who has gone in search of the kingdom of heaven the old hermit says: "I have lived here for three hundred years, but never yet has anybody asked me about the kingdom of heaven. I cannot tell you myself; but up there, on another floor of the house, live all kinds of birds, and they can surely tell you." [19] The old man knows what roads lead to the goal and points them out to the hero. [20] He warns of dangers to come and supplies the means of meeting them effectively. For instance, he tells the boy who has gone to fetch the silver water that the well is guarded by a lion who has the deceptive trick of sleeping with his eyes open and watching with his eyes shut; [21] or he counsels the youth who is riding to a magic fountain in order to fetch the healing draught for the king, only to draw the water at a trot because of the lurking witches who lasso everybody that comes to the fountain. [22] He charges the princess whose lover has been changed into a werewolf to make a fire and put a cauldron of tar over it. Then she must plunge her beloved white lily into the boiling tar, and when the werewolf comes, she must empty the cauldron over its head, which will release her lover from the spell. [23] Occasionally the old man is a very critical old man, as in the Caucasian tale of the youngest prince who wanted to build a flawless church for his father, so as to inherit the kingdom. This he does, and nobody can discover a single flaw, but then an old man comes along and says, "That's a fine church you've built, to be sure! What a pity the main wall is a bit crooked!" The prince has the church pulled down again

18 *Finnische und estnische Volksmärchen,* loc. cit.
19 *Deutsche Märchen seit Grimm,* p. 382 [op. cit.]. In one Balkan tale (*Balkanmärchen,* p. 65 ["The Shepherd and the Three Samovilas"]) the old man is called the "Czar of all the birds." Here the magpie knows all the answers. Cf. the mysterious "master of the dovecot" in Gustav Meyrink's novel *Der weisse Dominikaner.*
20 *Märchen aus Iran,* p. 152 [op. cit.].
21 *Spanische und Portugiesische Märchen,* p. 158 ["The White Parrot"].
22 Ibid., p. 199 ["Queen Rose, or Little Tom"].
23 *Nordische Volksmärchen,* Vol. I, p. 231f. ["The Werewolf"].

and builds a new one, but here too the old man discovers a flaw, and so on for the third time.[24]

406   The old man thus represents knowledge, reflection, insight, wisdom, cleverness, and intuition on the one hand, and on the other, moral qualities such as goodwill and readiness to help, which make his "spiritual" character sufficiently plain. Since the archetype is an autonomous content of the unconscious, the fairytale, which usually concretizes the archetypes, can cause the old man to appear in a dream in much the same way as happens in modern dreams. In a Balkan tale the old man appears to the hard-pressed hero in a dream and gives him good advice about accomplishing the impossible tasks that have been imposed upon him.[25] His relation to the unconscious is clearly expressed in one Russian fairytale, where he is called the "King of the Forest." As the peasant sat down wearily on a tree stump, a little old man crept out: "all wrinkled he was and a green beard hung down to his knees." "Who are you?" asked the peasant. "I am Och, King of the Forest," said the manikin. The peasant hired out his profligate son to him, "and the King of the Forest departed with the young man, and conducted him to that other world under the earth and brought him to a green hut. . . . In the hut everything was green: the walls were green and the benches, Och's wife was green and the children were green . . . and the little water-women who waited on him were as green as rue." Even the food was green. The King of the Forest is here a vegetation or tree numen who reigns in the woods and, through the nixies, also has connections with water, which clearly shows his relation to the unconscious since the latter is frequently expressed through wood and water symbols.

407   There is equally a connection with the unconscious when the old man appears as a dwarf. The fairytale about the princess who was searching for her lover says: "Night came and the darkness, and still the princess sat in the same place and wept. As she sat there lost in thought, she heard a voice greeting her: 'Good evening, pretty maid! Why are you sitting here so lonely and sad?' She sprang up hastily and felt very confused, and that was no wonder. But when she looked round there was only a tiny little old man standing before her, who nodded his head at her

[24] *Kaukasische Märchen*, pp. 35f. ["The False and the True Nightingale"].
[25] *Balkanmärchen*, p. 217 ["The Lubi (She-Devil) and the Fair of the Earth"].

and looked so kind and simple." In a Swiss fairytale, the peasant's son who wants to bring the king's daughter a basket of apples encounters "es chlis isigs Männdli, das frogt-ne, was er do i dem Chratte häig?" (a little iron man who asked what he had there in the basket). In another passage the "Männdli" has "es isigs Chlaidli a" (iron clothes on). By "isig" presumably "eisern" (iron) is meant, which is more probable than "eisig" (icy). In the latter case it would have to be "es Chlaidli vo Is" (clothes of ice).[26] There are indeed little ice men, and little metal men too; in fact, in a modern dream I have even come across a little black iron man who appeared at a critical juncture, like the one in this fairytale of the country bumpkin who wanted to marry the princess.

408   In a modern series of visions in which the figure of the wise old man occurred several times, he was on one occasion of normal size and appeared at the very bottom of a crater surrounded by high rocky walls; on another occasion he was a tiny figure on the top of a mountain, inside a low, stony enclosure. We find the same motif in Goethe's tale of the dwarf princess who lived in a casket.[27] In this connection we might also mention the Anthroparion, the little leaden man of the Zosimos vision,[28] as well as the metallic men who dwell in the mines, the crafty dactyls of antiquity, the homunculi of the alchemists, and the gnomic throng of hobgoblins, brownies, gremlins, etc. How "real" such conceptions are became clear to me on the occasion of a serious mountaineering accident: after the catastrophe two of the climbers had the collective vision, in broad daylight, of a little hooded man who scrambled out of an inaccessible crevasse in the ice face and passed across the glacier, creating a regular panic in the two beholders. I have often encountered motifs which made me think that the unconscious must be the world of the infinitesimally small. Such an idea could be derived rationalistically from the obscure feeling that in all these visions we are dealing with something endopsychic, the inference being that a thing must be exceedingly small in order to fit

---

26 This occurs in the tale of the griffin, No. 84 in the volume of children's fairytales collected by the brothers Grimm (1912), II, pp. 84ff. The text swarms with phonetic mistakes. [The English text (trans. by Margaret Hunt, rev. by James Stern, no. 165) has "hoary."—TRANS.]   27 Goethe, "Die neue Melusine."
28 Cf. "The Visions of Zosimos," par. 87 (III, i, 2–3).

inside the head. I am no friend of any such "rational" conjectures, though I would not say that they are all beside the mark. It seems to me more probable that this liking for diminutives on the one hand and for superlatives—giants, etc.—on the other is connected with the queer uncertainty of spatial and temporal relations in the unconscious.[29] Man's sense of proportion, his rational conception of big and small, is distinctly anthropomorphic, and it loses its validity not only in the realm of physical phenomena but also in those parts of the collective unconscious beyond the range of the specifically human. The atman is "smaller than small and bigger than big," he is "the size of a thumb" yet he "encompasses the earth on every side and rules over the ten-finger space." And of the Cabiri Goethe says: "little in length / mighty in strength." In the same way, the archetype of the wise old man is quite tiny, almost imperceptible, and yet it possesses a fateful potency, as anyone can see when he gets down to fundamentals. The archetypes have this peculiarity in common with the atomic world, which is demonstrating before our eyes that the more deeply the investigator penetrates into the universe of microphysics the more devastating are the explosive forces he finds enchained there. That the greatest effects come from the smallest causes has become patently clear not only in physics but in the field of psychological research as well. How often in the critical moments of life everything hangs on what appears to be a mere nothing!

409   In certain primitive fairytales, the illuminating quality of our archetype is expressed by the fact that the old man is identified with the sun. He brings a firebrand with him which he uses for roasting a pumpkin. After he has eaten, he takes the fire away again, which causes mankind to steal it from him.[30] In a North American Indian tale, the old man is a witch-doctor who owns the fire.[31] Spirit too has a fiery aspect, as we know from the language of the Old Testament and from the story of the Pentecostal miracle.

[29] In one Siberian fairytale (*Märchen aus Sibirien*, no. 13 ["The Man Turned to Stone"]) the old man is a white shape towering up to heaven.
[30] *Indianermärchen aus Südamerika*, p. 285 ["The End of the World and the Theft of Fire"—Bolivian].
[31] *Indianermärchen aus Nordamerika*, p. 74 [Tales of Manabos: "The Theft of Fire"].

THE SPIRIT MERCURIUS

Part I

1. THE SPIRIT IN THE BOTTLE

In my contribution[1] to the symposium on Hermes I will try to show that this many-hued and wily god did not by any means die with the decline of the classical era, but on the contrary has gone on living in strange guises through the centuries, even into recent times, and has kept the mind of man busy with his deceptive arts and healing gifts. Children are still told Grimm's fairytale of "The Spirit in the Bottle," which is ever-living like all fairytales, and moreover contains the quintessence and deepest meaning of the Hermetic mystery as it has come down to us today:

Once upon a time there was a poor woodcutter. He had an only son, whom he wished to send to a high school. However, since he could give him only a little money to take with him, it was used up long before the time for the examinations. So the son went home and helped his father with the work in the forest. Once, during the midday rest, he roamed the woods and came to an immense old oak. There he heard a voice calling from the ground, "Let me out, let me out!" He dug down among the roots of the tree and found a well-sealed glass bottle from which, clearly, the voice had come. He opened it and instantly a spirit rushed out and soon became half as high as the tree. The spirit cried in an awful voice: "I have had my punishment and I will be revenged! I am the great and mighty spirit Mercurius, and now you shall have your reward. Whoso releases me, him I must strangle." This made the boy uneasy and, quickly thinking up a trick, he said, "First, I must be sure that you are the same spirit that was shut up in that little bottle." To prove this, the spirit crept back into the bottle. Then the boy made haste to seal it and the spirit was caught again. But now the spirit promised to reward him richly if the boy would let

[1] I give only a general survey of the Mercurius concept in alchemy and by no means an exhaustive exposition of it. The illustrative material cited should therefore be taken only as examples and makes no claim to completeness. [For the "symposium on Hermes" see the editorial note on p. 191.—EDITORS.]

him out. So he let him out and received as a reward a small piece of rag. Quoth the spirit: "If you spread one end of this over a wound it will heal, and if you rub steel or iron with the other end it will turn into silver." Thereupon the boy rubbed his damaged axe with the rag, and the axe turned to silver and he was able to sell it for four hundred thaler. Thus father and son were freed from all worries. The young man could return to his studies, and later, thanks to his rag, he became a famous doctor.[2]

240   Now, what insight can we gain from this fairytale? As you know, we can treat fairytales as fantasy products, like dreams, conceiving them to be spontaneous statements of the unconscious about itself.

241   As at the beginning of many dreams something is said about the scene of the dream action, so the fairytale mentions the forest as the place of the magic happening. The forest, dark and impenetrable to the eye, like deep water and the sea, is the container of the unknown and the mysterious. It is an appropriate synonym for the unconscious. Among the many trees—the living elements that make up the forest—one tree is especially conspicuous for its great size. Trees, like fishes in the water, represent the living contents of the unconscious. Among these contents one of special significance is characterized as an "oak." Trees have individuality. A tree, therefore, is often a symbol of personality.[3] Ludwig II of Bavaria is said to have honoured certain particularly impressive trees in his park by having them saluted. The mighty old oak is proverbially the king of the forest. Hence it represents a central figure among the contents of the unconscious, possessing personality in the most marked degree. It is the prototype of the *self*, a symbol of the source and goal of the individuation process. The oak stands for the still unconscious core of the personality, the plant symbolism indicating a state of deep unconsciousness. From this it may be concluded that the hero of the fairytale is profoundly unconscious of himself. He is one of the "sleepers," the "blind" or "blindfolded," whom we

2 [Author's paraphrase. Cf. "The Spirit in the Bottle," *Grimm's Fairy Tales* (trans. Hunt, rev. Stern), pp. 458–62.—EDITORS.]
3 Concerning personification of trees, see Frazer, *The Magic Art,* II, ch. 9. Trees are also the dwelling places of spirits of the dead or are identical with the life of the newborn child (ibid., I, p. 184).

encounter in the illustrations of certain alchemical treatises.[4] They are the unawakened who are still unconscious of themselves, who have not yet integrated their future, more extensive personality, their "wholeness," or, in the language of the mystics, the ones who are not yet "enlightened." For our hero, therefore, the tree conceals a great secret.[5]

242   The secret is hidden not in the top but in the roots of the tree;[6] and since it is,' or has, a personality it also possesses the most striking marks of personality—voice, speech, and conscious purpose, and it demands to be set free by the hero. It is caught and imprisoned against its will, down there in the earth among the roots of the tree. The roots extend into the inorganic realm, into the mineral kingdom. In psychological terms, this would mean that the self has its roots in the body, indeed in the body's chemical elements. Whatever this remarkable statement of the fairytale may mean in itself, it is in no way stranger than the miracle of the living plant rooted in the inanimate earth. The alchemists described their four elements as *radices*, corresponding to the Empedoclean *rhizomata*, and in them they saw the constituents of the most significant and central symbol of alchemy, the *lapis philosophorum*, which represents the goal of the individuation process.

243   The secret hidden in the roots is a spirit sealed inside a bottle. Naturally it was not hidden away among the roots to start with, but was first confined in a bottle, which was then hidden. Presumably a magician, that is, an alchemist, caught and imprisoned it. As we shall see later, this spirit is something like the numen of the tree, its *spiritus vegetativus*, which is one

4 Cf. the title-page of *Mutus liber*, showing an angel waking the sleeper with a trumpet ("The Psychology of the Transference," Fig. 11). Also the illustration in Michelspacher's *Cabala, speculum artis et naturae* (*Psychology and Alchemy*, Fig. 93). In the foreground, before a mountain upon which is a temple of the initiates, stands a blindfolded man, while further back another man runs after a fox which is disappearing into a hole in the mountain. The "helpful animal" shows the way to the temple. The fox or hare is itself the "evasive" Mercurius as guide (ὁδηγός).

5 For additional material on the tree symbol, see infra, "The Philosophical Tree," Part II.

6 This motif was used in the same sense by the Gnostics. Cf. Hippolytus, *Elenchos*, V, 9, 15, where the many-named and thousand-eyed "Word of God" is "hidden in the root of All."

definition of Mercurius. As the life principle of the tree, it is a sort of spiritual quintessence abstracted from it, and could also be described as the *principium individuationis*. The tree would then be the outward and visible sign of the realization of the self. The alchemists appear to have held a similar view. Thus the "Aurelia occulta" says: "The philosophers have sought most eagerly for the centre of the tree which stands in the midst of the earthly paradise." [7] According to the same source, Christ himself is this tree.[8] The tree comparison occurs as early as Eulogius of Alexandria (c. A.D. 600), who says: "Behold in the Father the root, in the Son the branch, and in the Spirit the fruit: for the substance [οὐσία] in the three is one." [9] Mercurius, too, is *trinus et unus*.

244   So if we translate it into psychological language, the fairytale tells us that the mercurial essence, the *principium individuationis*, would have developed freely under natural conditions, but was robbed of its freedom by deliberate intervention from outside, and was artfully confined and banished like an evil spirit. (Only evil spirits have to be confined, and the wickedness of this spirit was shown by its murderous intent.) Supposing the fairytale is right and the spirit was really as wicked as it relates, we would have to conclude that the Master who imprisoned the *principium individuationis* had a good end in view. But who is this well-intentioned Master who has the power to banish the principle of man's individuation? Such power is given only to a ruler of souls in the spiritual realm. The idea that the principle of individuation is the source of all evil is found in Schopenhauer and still more in Buddhism. In Christianity, too, human nature is tainted with original sin and is redeemed from this stain by Christ's self-sacrifice. Man in his "natural" condition is neither good nor pure, and if he should develop in the natural way the result would be a product not essentially different from an animal. Sheer instinctuality and naïve unconsciousness untroubled by a sense of guilt would prevail if the Master had not interrupted the free development of the natural being by introducing a distinction between good and evil and outlawing the evil. Since without guilt there is no moral consciousness and

[7] *Theatrum chemicum*, IV (1659), p. 500.
[8] Ibid., p. 478: "(Christ), who is the tree of life both spiritual and bodily."
[9] Krueger, *Das Dogma von der Dreieinigkeit und Gottmenschheit*, p. 207.

without awareness of differences no consciousness at all, we must concede that the strange intervention of the master of souls was absolutely necessary for the development of any kind of consciousness and in this sense was for the good. According to our religious beliefs, God himself is this Master—and the alchemist, in his small way, competes with the Creator in so far as he strives to do work analogous to the work of creation, and therefore he likens his microcosmic opus to the work of the world creator.[10]

245   In our fairytale the natural evil is banished to the "roots," that is, to the earth, in other words the body. This statement agrees with the historical fact that Christian thought in general has held the body in contempt, without bothering much about the finer doctrinal distinctions.[11] For, according to doctrine, neither the body nor nature in general is evil *per se:* as the work of God, or as the actual form in which he manifests himself, nature cannot be identical with evil. Correspondingly, the evil spirit in the fairytale is not simply banished to the earth and allowed to roam about at will, but is only hidden there in a safe and special container, so that he cannot call attention to himself anywhere except right under the oak. The bottle is an artificial human product and thus signifies the intellectual purposefulness and artificiality of the procedure, whose obvious aim is to isolate the spirit from the surrounding medium. As the *vas Hermeticum* of alchemy, it was "hermetically" sealed (i.e., sealed with the sign of Hermes);[12] it had to be made of glass, and had also to be as round as possible, since it was meant to represent the cosmos in which the earth was created.[13] Transparent glass is something like solidified water or air, both of which are synonyms for spirit. The alchemical retort is therefore equivalent to the *anima mundi,* which according to an old alchemical conception surrounds the cosmos. Caesarius of Heisterbach (thirteenth century) mentions a vision in which the soul appeared as a

---

10 In the "Dicta Belini" Mercurius even says: "Out of me is made the bread from which comes the whole world, and the world is formed from my mercy, and it fails not, because it is the gift of God" (Distinctio XXVIII, in *Theatr. chem.,* V, 1660, p. 87).

11 Cf. the doctrine of the *status iustitiae originalis* and *status naturae integrae.*

12 Cf. Rev. 20 : 3: "and set a seal upon him."

13 "The Fift is of Concord and of Love, / Betweene your Warkes and the Spheare above."—Norton's "Ordinall of Alchimy," *Theatrum chemicum Britannicum,* ch. 6, p. 92.

spherical glass vessel.[14] Likewise the "spiritual" or "ethereal" (*aethereus*) philosophers' stone is a precious *vitrum* (sometimes described as *malleabile*) which was often equated with the gold glass (*aurum vitreum*) of the heavenly Jerusalem (Rev. 21 : 21).

246   It is worth noting that the German fairytale calls the spirit confined in the bottle by the name of the pagan god, Mercurius, who was considered identical with the German national god, Wotan. The mention of Mercurius stamps the fairytale as an alchemical folk legend, closely related on the one hand to the allegorical tales used in teaching alchemy, and on the other to the well-known group of folktales that cluster round the motif of the "spellbound spirit." Our fairytale thus interprets the evil spirit as a pagan god, forced under the influence of Christianity to descend into the dark underworld and be morally disqualified. Hermes becomes the demon of the mysteries celebrated by all *tenebriones* (obscurantists), and Wotan the demon of forest and storm; Mercurius becomes the soul of the metals, the metallic man (*homunculus*), the dragon (*serpens mercurialis*), the roaring fiery lion, the night raven (*nycticorax*), and the black eagle—the last four being synonyms for the devil. In fact the spirit in the bottle behaves just as the devil does in many other fairytales: he bestows wealth by changing base metal into gold; and like the devil, he also gets tricked.

[14] *Dialogus miraculorum,* trans. by Scott and Bland, I, pp. 42, 236.

2. THE CONNECTION BETWEEN
SPIRIT AND TREE

247   Before continuing our discussion of the spirit Mercurius, I should like to point out a not unimportant fact. The place where he lies confined is not just any place but a very essential one—namely, under the oak, the king of the forest. In psychological terms, this means that the evil spirit is imprisoned in the roots of the self, as the secret hidden in the principle of individuation. He is not identical with the tree, nor with its roots, but has been put there by artificial means. The fairytale gives us no reason to think that the oak, which represents the self, has grown out of the spirit in the bottle; we may rather conjecture that the oak presented a suitable place for concealing a secret. A treasure, for instance, is preferably buried near some kind of landmark, or else such a mark is put up afterwards. The tree of paradise serves as a prototype for this and similar tales: it, too, is not identical with the voice of the serpent which issued from it.[1] However, it must not be forgotten that these mythical motifs have a significant connection with certain psychological phenomena observed among primitive peoples. In all such cases there is a notable analogy with primitive animism: certain trees are animated by souls—have the character of personality, we would say—and possess a voice that gives commands to human beings. Amaury Talbot[2] reports one such case from Nigeria, where a native soldier heard an *oji* tree calling to him, and tried desperately to break out of the barracks and hasten to the tree. Under cross-examination he alleged that all those who bore the name of the tree now and then heard its voice. Here the voice is undoubtedly identical with the tree. These psychic phenomena

---

1 Mercurius, in the form of Lilith or Melusina, appears in the tree in the Ripley *Scrowle*. To this context belongs also the hamadryad as an interpretation of the so-called "Aenigma Bononiense." Cf. *Mysterium Coniunctionis*, pp. 68f.
2 *In the Shadow of the Bush*, pp. 31f.

suggest that originally the tree and the daemon were one and the same, and that their separation is a secondary phenomenon corresponding to a higher level of culture and consciousness. The original phenomenon was nothing less than a nature deity, a *tremendum* pure and simple, which is morally neutral. But the secondary phenomenon implies an act of discrimination which splits man off from nature and thus testifies to the existence of a more highly differentiated consciousness. To this is added, as a tertiary phenomenon testifying to a still higher level, the moral qualification which declares the voice to be an evil spirit under a ban. It goes without saying that this third level is marked by a belief in a "higher" and "good" God who, though he has not finally disposed of his adversary, has nevertheless rendered him harmless for some time to come by imprisonment (Rev. 20 : 1–3).

248   Since at the present level of consciousness we cannot suppose that tree daemons exist, we are forced to assert that the primitive suffers from hallucinations, that he hears his own unconscious which has projected itself into the tree. If this theory is correct—and I do not know how we could formulate it otherwise today—then the second level of consciousness has effected a differentiation between the object "tree" and the unconscious content projected into it, thereby achieving an act of enlightenment. The third level rises still higher and attributes "evil" to the psychic content which has been separated from the object. Finally a fourth level, the level reached by our consciousness today, carries the enlightenment a stage further by denying the objective existence of the "spirit" and declaring that the primitive has heard nothing at all, but merely had an auditory hallucination. Consequently the whole phenomenon vanishes into thin air—with the great advantage that the evil spirit becomes obviously non-existent and sinks into ridiculous insignificance. A fifth level, however, which is bound to take a quintessential view of the matter, wonders about this conjuring trick that turns what began as a miracle into a senseless self-deception—only to come full circle. Like the boy who told his father a made-up story about sixty stags in the forest, it asks: "But what, then, was all the rustling in the woods?" The fifth level is of the opinion that something did happen after all: even though the psychic content was not the tree, nor a spirit in the tree, nor indeed any spirit at

all, it was nevertheless a phenomenon thrusting up from the unconscious, the existence of which cannot be denied if one is minded to grant the psyche any kind of reality. If one did not do that, one would have to extend God's *creatio ex nihilo*—which seems so obnoxious to the modern intellect—very much further to include steam engines, automobiles, radios, and every library on earth, all of which would presumably have arisen from unimaginably fortuitous conglomerations of atoms. The only thing that would have happened is that the Creator would have been renamed Conglomeratio.

249   The fifth level assumes that the unconscious exists and has a reality just like any other existent. However odious it may be, this means that the "spirit" is also a reality, and the "evil" spirit at that. What is even worse, the distinction between "good" and "evil" is suddenly no longer obsolete, but highly topical and necessary. The crucial point is that so long as the evil spirit cannot be proved to be a subjective psychic experience, then even trees and other suitable objects would have, once again, to be seriously considered as its lodging places.

3. THE PROBLEM OF FREEING MERCURIUS

We will not pursue the paradoxical reality of the unconscious any further now, but will return to the fairytale of the spirit in the bottle. As we have seen, the spirit Mercurius bears some resemblance to the "cheated devil." The analogy, however, is only a superficial one, since, unlike the gifts of the devil, the gold of Mercurius does not turn to horse droppings but remains good metal, and the magic rag does not turn to ashes by morning but retains its healing power. Nor is Mercurius tricked out of a soul that he wanted to steal. He is only tricked into his own better nature, one might say, in that the boy succeeds in bottling him up again in order to cure his bad mood and make him tractable. Mercurius becomes polite, gives the young fellow a useful ransom and is accordingly set free. We now hear about the student's good fortune and how he became a wonder-working doctor, but—strangely enough—nothing about the doings of the liberated spirit, though these might be of some interest in view of the web of meanings in which Mercurius, with his many-sided associations, entangles us. What happens when this pagan god, Hermes-Mercurius-Wotan, is let loose again? Being a god of magicians, a *spiritus vegetativus,* and a storm daemon, he will hardly have returned to captivity, and the fairytale gives us no reason to suppose that the episode of imprisonment has finally changed his nature to the pink of perfection. The bird of Hermes has escaped from the glass cage, and in consequence something has happened which the experienced alchemist wished at all costs to avoid. That is why he always sealed the stopper of his bottle with magic signs and set it for a very long time over the lowest fire, so that "he who is within may not fly out." For if he escapes, the whole laborious opus comes to nothing and has to be started all over again. Our lad was a Sunday's child and possibly one of the poor in spirit, on whom was bestowed a bit of the Kingdom of Heaven in the shape of the self-renewing tincture, with reference to which it was said that the opus needed to be performed only once.[1] But if he had lost the magic rag he would certainly never have been able to produce it a second time, by himself. It looks as though some Master had succeeded in capturing the mercurial spirit and then hid him in a safe place, like a treasure—perhaps putting him aside for some future use. He may even have planned to tame the wild Mercurius to serve him as a willing "familiar," like Mephisto—such trains of thought are not strange to alchemy. Perhaps he was disagreeably surprised when he returned to the oak tree and found that his bird had flown. At any rate, it might have been better not to have left the fate of the bottle to chance.

251   Be that as it may, the behaviour of the boy—successfully as it worked out for him—must be described as alchemically incorrect. Apart from the fact that he may have infringed upon the legitimate claims of an unknown Master by setting Mercurius free, he was also totally unconscious of what might follow if this turbulent spirit were let loose upon the world. The golden age of alchemy was the sixteenth and the first half of the seventeenth century. At that time a storm bird did indeed escape from a spiritual vessel which the daemons must have felt was a prison. As I have said, the alchemists were all for not letting Mercurius escape. They wanted to keep him in the bottle in order to transform him: for they believed, like Petasios, that lead (another arcane substance) was "so bedevilled and shameless that all who wish to investigate it fall into madness through ignorance." [2] The same was said of the elusive Mercurius who evades every grasp—a real trickster who drove the alchemists to despair.[3]

---

1 "For he that shall end it once for certeyne, / Shall never have neede to begin againe."—Norton's "Ordinall of Alchimy," *Theatr. chem. Brit.*, ch. 4, p. 48.
2 Olympiodorus in Berthelot, *Alchimistes grecs*, II, iv, 43.
3 Cf. the entertaining "Dialogus Mercurii alchymistae et naturae," in *Theatr. chem.*, IV (1659), pp. 449ff.

10. SUMMARY

284   The multiple aspects of Mercurius may be summarized as follows:

(1) Mercurius consists of all conceivable opposites. He is thus quite obviously a duality, but is named a unity in spite of the fact that his innumerable inner contradictions can dramatically fly apart into an equal number of disparate and apparently independent figures.

(2) He is both material and spiritual.

(3) He is the process by which the lower and material is transformed into the higher and spiritual, and vice versa.

(4) He is the devil, a redeeming psychopomp, an evasive trickster, and God's reflection in physical nature.

(5) He is also the reflection of a mystical experience of the artifex that coincides with the *opus alchymicum*.

(6) As such, he represents on the one hand the self and on the other the individuation process and, because of the limitless number of his names, also the collective unconscious.[1]

***

285   Certainly goldmaking, as also chemical research in general, was of great concern to alchemy. But a still greater, more impassioned concern appears to have been—one cannot very well say the "investigation"—but rather the *experience* of the unconscious. That this side of alchemy—the μυστικά—was for so long misunderstood is due solely to the fact that nothing was known of psychology, let alone of the suprapersonal, collective unconscious. So long as one knows nothing of psychic actuality, it will be projected, if it appears at all. Thus the first knowledge of psychic law and order was found in the stars, and was later extended by projections into unknown matter. These two realms of experience branched off into sciences: astrology became astron-

---

1 Hence the designation of Mercurius as *mare nostrum*.

omy, and alchemy chemistry. On the other hand, the peculiar connection between character and the astronomical determination of time has only very recently begun to turn into something approaching an empirical science. The really important psychic facts can neither be measured, weighed, nor seen in a test tube or under a microscope. They are therefore supposedly indeterminable, in other words they must be left to people who have an inner sense for them, just as colours must be shown to the seeing and not to the blind.

286   The store of projections found in alchemy is, if possible, even less known, and there is a further drawback which makes closer investigation extremely difficult. For, unlike the astrological constituents of character which, if negative, are at most unpleasant for the individual, though amusing to his neighbour, the alchemical projections represent collective contents that stand in painful contrast—or rather, in compensatory relation— to our highest rational convictions and values. They give the strange answers of the natural psyche to the ultimate questions which reason has left untouched. Contrary to all progress and belief in a future that will deliver us from the sorrowful present, they point back to something primeval, to the apparently hopelessly static, eternal sway of matter that makes our fondly believed-in world look like a phantasmagoria of shifting scenes. They show us, as the redemptive goal of our active, desirous life, a symbol of the inorganic—the stone—something that does not live but merely exists or "becomes," the passive subject of a limitless and unfathomable play of opposites. "Soul," that bodiless abstraction of the rational intellect, and "spirit," that twodimensional metaphor of dry-as-dust philosophical dialectic, appear in alchemical projection in almost physical, plastic form, like tangible breath-bodies, and refuse to function as component parts of our rational consciousness. The hope for a psychology without the soul is brought to nothing, and the illusion that the unconscious has only just been discovered vanishes: in a somewhat peculiar form, admittedly, it has been known for close on two thousand years. Let us, however, not delude ourselves: no more than we can separate the constituents of character from the astronomical determinants of time are we able to separate that unruly and evasive Mercurius from the autonomy of matter. Something of the projection-carrier always clings to the projec-

tion, and even if we succeed to some degree in integrating into our consciousness the part we recognize as psychic, we shall integrate along with it something of the cosmos and its materiality; or rather, since the cosmos is infinitely greater than we are, we shall have been assimilated by the inorganic. "Transform yourselves into living philosophical stones!" cries an alchemist, but he did not know how infinitely slowly the stone "becomes." Anyone who gives serious thought to the "natural light" that emanates from the projections of alchemy will certainly agree with the Master who spoke of the "wearisomeness of the interminable meditation" demanded by the work. In these projections we encounter the phenomenology of an "objective" spirit, a true matrix of psychic experience, the most appropriate symbol for which is matter. Nowhere and never has man controlled matter without closely observing its behaviour and paying heed to its laws, and only to the extent that he did so could he control it. The same is true of that objective spirit which today we call the unconscious: it is refractory like matter, mysterious and elusive, and obeys laws which are so non-human or suprahuman that they seem to us like a *crimen laesae majestatis humanae*. If a man puts his hand to the opus, he repeats, as the alchemists say, God's work of creation. The struggle with the unformed, with the chaos of Tiamat, is in truth a primordial experience.

287   Since the psyche, when directly experienced, confronts us in the "living" substance it has animated and appears to be one with it, Mercurius is called *argentum vivum*. Conscious discrimination, or consciousness itself, effects that world-shattering intervention which separates body from soul and divides the spirit Mercurius from the *hydrargyrum*, as if drawing off the spirit into the bottle, to speak in terms of our fairytale. But since body and soul, in spite of the artificial separation, are united in the mystery of life, the mercurial spirit, though imprisoned in the bottle, is yet found in the roots of the tree, as its quintessence and living numen. In the language of the Upanishads, he is the personal atman of the tree. Isolated in the bottle, he corresponds to the ego and the principle of individuation, which in the Indian view leads to the illusion of individual existence. Freed from his prison, Mercurius assumes the character of the suprapersonal atman. He becomes the *one* animating principle of all

created things, the *hiranyagarbha* (golden germ),[2] the supra-personal self, represented by the *filius macrocosmi*, the *one* stone of the wise. "Rosinus ad Sarratantam" cites a saying of "Malus Philosophus"[3] which attempts to formulate the psychological relation of the lapis to consciousness: "This stone is below thee, as to obedience; above thee, as to dominion; therefore from thee, as to knowledge; about thee, as to equals."[4] Applied to the self, this would mean: "The self is subordinate to you, yet on the other hand rules you. It is dependent on your own efforts and your knowledge, but transcends you and embraces all those who are of like mind." This refers to the collective nature of the self, since the self epitomizes the wholeness of the personality. By definition, wholeness includes the collective unconscious, which as experience seems to show is everywhere identical.

288   The encounter of the poor student with the spirit in the bottle portrays the spiritual adventure of a blind and unawakened human being. The same motif underlies the tale of the swine-herd who climbed the world-tree,[5] and also forms the *leitmotiv* of alchemy. For what it signifies is the individuation process as it prepares itself in the unconscious and gradually enters consciousness. The commonest alchemical symbol for this is the tree, the *arbor philosophica,* which derives from the paradisal tree of knowledge. Here, as in our fairytale, a daemonic serpent, an evil spirit, prods and persuades to knowledge. In view of the Biblical precedent, it is not surprising that the spirit Mercurius has, to say the least, a great many connections with the dark side. One of his aspects is the female serpent-daemon, Lilith or Melusina, who lives in the philosophical tree. At the same time, he not only partakes of the Holy Spirit but, according to alchemy, is actually identical with it. We have no choice but to accept this shocking paradox after all we have learnt about the ambivalence of the spirit archetype. Our ambiguous Mercurius simply con-

2 Cf. Maitrayana-Brāhmana Upanishad, V, 8 (Sacred Books of the East, vol. 15, p. 311). He occurs as the *spiritus vegetativus* and collective soul in the Vedanta-Sutras (ibid., vol. 34, p. 173, and vol. 48, p. 578).
3 The treatise of Rosinus (Zosimos) is probably of Arabic origin. "Malus" might be a corruption of "Magus." The *Fihrist* of Ibn al-Nadim (A.D. 987) lists, along with writings of Rimas (Zosimos), two works by Magus one of which is entitled "The Book of the Wise Magus (?) on the Art" (Ruska, *Turba,* p. 272).
4 *Art. aurif.,* I, p. 310.
5 Cf. "The Phenomenology of the Spirit in Fairytales," pp. 231ff.

firms the rule. In any case, the paradox is no worse than the Creator's whimsical notion of enlivening his peaceful, innocent paradise with the presence of an obviously rather dangerous tree-snake, "accidentally" located on the very same tree as the forbidden apples.

289   It must be admitted that the fairytale and alchemy both show Mercurius in a predominantly unfavourable light, which is all the more striking because his positive aspect relates him not only to the Holy Spirit, but, in the form of the lapis, also to Christ and, as a triad, even to the Trinity. It looks as if it were precisely these relationships which led the alchemists to put particular stress on the dark and dubious quality of Mercurius, and this militates strongly against the assumption that by their lapis they really meant Christ. If this had been their meaning, why should they have renamed Christ the *lapis philosophorum?* The lapis is at most a counterpart or analogy of Christ in the physical world. Its symbolism, like that of Mercurius who constitutes its substance, points, psychologically speaking, to the self, as also does the symbolic figure of Christ.[6] In comparison with the purity and unity of the Christ symbol, Mercurius-lapis is ambiguous, dark, paradoxical, and thoroughly pagan. It therefore represents a part of the psyche which was certainly not moulded by Christianity and can on no account be expressed by the symbol "Christ." On the contrary, as we have seen, in many ways it points to the devil, who is known at times to disguise himself as an angel of light. The lapis formulates an aspect of the self which stands apart, bound to nature and at odds with the Christian spirit. It represents all those things which have been eliminated from the Christian model. But since they possess living reality, they cannot express themselves otherwise than in dark Hermetic symbols. The paradoxical nature of Mercurius reflects an important aspect of the self—the fact, namely, that it is essentially a *complexio oppositorum,* and indeed can be nothing else if it is to represent any kind of totality. Mercurius as *deus terrestris* has something of that *deus absconditus* (hidden god) which is an essential element of the psychological self, and the self cannot be distinguished from a God-image (except by incontestable and unprovable faith). Although I have stressed that the lapis is

6 [Cf. *Psychology and Alchemy,* ch. 5. "The Lapis-Christ Parallel," and *Aion,* ch. 5, "Christ, a Symbol of the Self."—EDITORS.]

a symbol embracing the opposites, it should not be thought of as a—so to speak—more complete symbol of the self. That would be decidedly incorrect, for actually it is an image whose form and content are largely determined by the unconscious. For this reason it is never found in the texts in finished and well-defined form; we have to combine all the scattered references to the various arcane substances, to Mercurius, to the transformation process and the end product. Although the lapis in one aspect or another is almost always the subject discussed, there is no real consensus of opinion in regard to its actual form. Almost every author has his own special allegories, synonyms, and metaphors. This makes it clear that the stone, though indeed an object of general experiment, was to an even greater extent an outcropping of the unconscious, which only sporadically crossed the borderline of subjectivity and gave rise to the vague general concept of the *lapis philosophorum*.

290   Opposed to this figure veiled in the twilight of more or less secret doctrines there stands, sharply outlined by dogma, the Son of Man and Salvator Mundi, Christ the Sol Novus, before whom the lesser stars pale. He is the affirmation of the daylight of consciousness in trinitarian form. So clear and definite is the Christ figure that whatever differs from him must appear not only inferior but perverse and vile. This is not the result of Christ's own teaching, but rather of what is taught about him, and especially of the crystal purity which dogma has bestowed upon his figure. As a result, a tension of opposites such as had never occurred before in the whole history of Christianity beginning with the Creation arose between Christ and the Antichrist, as Satan or the fallen angel. At the time of Job, Satan is still found among the sons of God. "Now there was a day," it says in Job 1 : 6, "when the sons of God came to present themselves before the Lord, and Satan came also among them." This picture of a celestial family reunion gives no hint of the New Testament "Get thee hence, Satan" (Matthew 4 : 10), nor yet of the dragon chained in the underworld for a thousand years (Rev. 20 : 2). It looks as if the superabundance of light on one side had produced an all the blacker darkness on the other. One can also see that the uncommonly great diffusion of black substance makes a sinless being almost impossible. A loving belief in such a being naturally involves cleansing one's own house of black filth. But the

filth must be dumped somewhere, and no matter where the dump lies it will plague even the best of all possible worlds with a bad smell.

291   The balance of the primordial world is upset. What I have said is not intended as a criticism, for I am deeply convinced not only of the relentless logic but of the expediency of this development. The emphatic differentiation of opposites is synonymous with sharper discrimination, and that is the *sine qua non* for any broadening or heightening of consciousness. The progressive differentiation of consciousness is the most important task of human biology and accordingly meets with the highest rewards— vastly increased chances of survival and the development of power technology. From the phylogenetic point of view, the effects of consciousness are as far-reaching as those of lung-breathing and warm-bloodedness. But clarification of consciousness necessarily entails an obscuration of those dimmer elements of the psyche which are less capable of becoming conscious, so that sooner or later a split occurs in the psychic system. Since it is not recognized as such it is projected, and appears in the form of a metaphysical split between the powers of light and the powers of darkness. The possibility of this projection is guaranteed by the presence of numerous archaic vestiges of the original daemons of light and darkness in any age. It seems likely, therefore, that the tension of opposites in Christianity is derived to a still unclarified degree from the dualism of ancient Persia, though the two are not identical.

292   There can be no doubt that the moral consequences of the Christian development represent a very considerable advance compared with the ancient Israelite religion of law. The Christianity of the synoptic gospels signifies little more than a coming to terms with issues inside Judaism, which may fairly be compared with the much earlier Buddhist reformation inside Hindu polytheism. Psychologically, both reformations resulted in a tremendous strengthening of consciousness. This is particularly evident in the maieutic method employed by Shakyamuni. But the sayings of Jesus manifest the same tendency, even if we discard as apocryphal the clearest formulation of this kind, the logion in Codex Bezae to Luke 6 : 4: "Man, if thou knowest what thou doest, thou art blessed. If thou knowest it not, thou art accursed and a transgressor of the law." At all events, the para-

ble of the unjust steward (Luke 16) has not found its way into the Apocrypha, where it would have fitted so well.

293   The rift in the metaphysical world has slowly risen into consciousness as a split in the human psyche, and the struggle between light and darkness moves to the battleground within. This shift of scene is not entirely self-evident, for which reason St. Ignatius Loyola considered it necessary to open our eyes to the conflict and impress it on our feelings by means of the most drastic spiritual exercises.[7] These efforts, for obvious reasons, had only a very limited range of application. And so, strangely enough, it was the medical men who, at the turn of the nineteenth century, were forced to intervene and get the obstructed process of conscious realization going again. Approaching the problem from a scientific angle, and innocent of any religious aim, Freud uncovered the abysmal darkness of human nature which a would-be enlightened optimism had striven to conceal. Since then psychotherapy, in one form or another, has persistently explored the extensive area of darkness which I have called the shadow. This attempt of modern science opened the eyes of only a few. However, the historic events of our time have painted a picture of man's psychic reality in indelible colours of blood and fire, and given him an object lesson which he will never be able to forget if—and this is the great question—he has today acquired enough consciousness to keep up with the furious pace of the devil within him. The only other hope is that he may learn to curb a creativity which is wasting itself in the exploitation of material power. Unfortunately, all attempts in that direction look like bloodless Utopias.

294   The figure of Christ the Logos has raised the *anima rationalis* in man to a level of importance which remains unobjectionable so long as it knows itself to be below and subject to the κύριος, the Lord of Spirits. Reason, however, has set itself free and proclaimed itself the ruler. It has sat enthroned in Notre Dame as Déesse Raison and heralded events that were to come. Our consciousness is no longer confined within a sacred temenos of otherworldly, eschatological images. It was helped to break free by a force that did not stream down from above—like the *lumen de lumine*—but came up with tremendous pressure from below and increased in strength as consciousness detached itself from the

7 *The Spiritual Exercises* (trans. Rickaby), pp. 75ff.

darkness and climbed into the light. In accordance with the principle of compensation which runs through the whole of nature, every psychic development, whether individual or collective, possesses an optimum which, when exceeded, produces an enantiodromia, that is, turns into its opposite. Compensatory tendencies emanating from the unconscious may be noted even during the approach to the critical turning-point, though if consciousness persists in its course they are completely repressed. The stirrings in the darkness necessarily seem like a devilish betrayal of the ideal of spiritual development. Reason cannot help condemning as unreasonable everything that contradicts it or deviates from its laws, in spite of all evidence to the contrary. Morality can permit itself no capacity for change, for whatever it does not agree with is inevitably immoral and has therefore to be repressed. It is not difficult to imagine the multitude of energies which must flow off into the unconscious under such conscious domination.

295 Hesitantly, as in a dream, the introspective brooding of the centuries gradually put together the figure of Mercurius and created a symbol which, according to all the psychological rules, stands in a compensatory relation to Christ. It is not meant to take his place, nor is it identical with him, for then indeed it could replace him. It owes its existence to the law of compensation, and its object is to throw a bridge across the abyss separating the two psychological worlds by presenting a subtle compensatory counterpoint to the Christ image. The fact that in *Faust* the compensatory figure is not, as one might almost have expected from the author's classical predilections, the wily messenger of the gods, but, as the name "Mephistopheles" [8] shows, a *familiaris* risen from the cesspits of medieval magic, proves, if anything, the ingrained Christian character of Goethe's consciousness. To the Christian mentality, the dark antagonist is always the devil. As I have shown, Mercurius escapes this prejudice by only a hair's breadth. But he escapes it, thanks to the fact that he scorns to carry on opposition at all costs. The magic of his name enables him, in spite of his ambiguity and duplicity, to keep outside the split, for as an ancient pagan god he possesses a natural undividedness which is impervious to logical and moral contradictions. This gives him invulnerability and incorrupti-

[8] [From L. *mephitis*, a noxious exhalation from the earth.—TRANSLATOR.]

bility, the very qualities we so urgently need to heal the split in ourselves.

296   If one makes a synopsis of all the descriptions and alchemical pictures of Mercurius, they form a striking parallel to the symbols of the self derived from other sources. One can hardly escape the conclusion that Mercurius as the lapis is a symbolic expression for the psychological complex which I have defined as the self. Similarly, the Christ figure must be viewed as a self symbol, and for the same reasons. But this leads to an apparently insoluble contradiction, for it is not at first clear how the unconscious can shape two such different images from one and the same content, which moreover possesses the character of totality. Certainly the centuries have done their spiritual work upon these two figures, and one is inclined to assume that both have been in large measure anthropomorphized during the process of assimilation. For those who hold that both figures are inventions of the intellect, the contradiction is quickly resolved. It then merely reflects the subjective psychic situation: the two figures would stand for man and his shadow.

297   This very simple and obvious solution is, unfortunately, founded on premises that do not stand up to criticism. The figures of Christ and the devil are both based on archetypal patterns, and were never invented but rather *experienced*. Their existence preceded all cognition of them,[9] and the intellect had no hand in the matter, except to assimilate them and if possible give them a place in its philosophy. Only the most superficial intellectualism can overlook this fundamental fact. We are actually confronted with two different images of the self, which in all likelihood presented a duality even in their original form. This duality was not invented, but is an autonomous phenomenon.

298   Since we naturally think from the standpoint of consciousness, we inevitably come to the conclusion that the split between consciousness and the unconscious is the sole cause of this duality. But experience has demonstrated the existence of a preconscious psychic functioning and of corresponding autonomous factors, the archetypes. Once we can accept the fact that the voices and delusions of the insane and the phobias and obsessions of the neurotic are beyond rational control, and that the ego cannot voluntarily fabricate dreams but simply dreams what

9 Evidence for this is the widespread motif of the two hostile brothers.

it has to, then we can also understand that the gods came first and theology later. Indeed, we must go a step further and assume that in the beginning there were two figures, one bright and one shadowy, and only afterwards did the light of consciousness detach itself from the night and the uncertain shimmer of its stars.

299   So if Christ and the dark nature-deity are autonomous images that can be directly experienced, we are obliged to reverse our rationalistic causal sequence, and instead of deriving these figures from our psychic conditions, must derive our psychic conditions from these figures. This is expecting a good deal of the modern intellect but does not alter the logic of our hypothesis. From this standpoint Christ appears as the archetype of consciousness and Mercurius as the archetype of the unconscious. As Cupid and Kyllenios, he tempts us out into the world of sense; he is the *benedicta viriditas* and the *multi flores* of early spring, a god of illusion and delusion of whom it is rightly said: "Invenitur in vena / Sanguine plena" (He is found in the vein swollen with blood). He is at the same time a Hermes Chthonios and an Eros, yet it is from him that there issues the "light surpassing all lights," the *lux moderna,* for the lapis is none other than the figure of light veiled in matter.[10] It is in this sense that St. Augustine quotes I Thessalonians 5 : 5, "Ye are all the children of light, and the children of the day: we are not of the night, nor of darkness," and distinguishes two forms of knowledge, a *cognitio vespertina* and a *cognitio matutina,* the first corresponding to the *scientia creaturae* and the second to the *scientia Creatoris.*[11] If we equate *cognitio* with consciousness, then Augustine's thought would suggest that the merely human and natural consciousness gradually darkens, as at nightfall. But just as evening gives birth to morning, so from the darkness arises a new light, the *stella matutina,* which is at once the evening and the morning star—Lucifer, the light-bringer.

300   Mercurius is by no means the Christian devil—the latter

10 Cf. the saying of Ostanes concerning the stone that has a spirit.
11 "For the knowledge of the creature, in comparison with the knowledge of the Creator, is but a twilight; and so it dawns and breaks into morning when the creature is drawn to the love and praise of the Creator. Nor is it ever darkened, save when the Creator is abandoned by the love of the creature."—*The City of God,* XI, vii.

could rather be said to be a "diabolization" of Lucifer or of Mercurius. Mercurius is an adumbration of the primordial light-bringer, who is never himself the light, but a φωσφόρος who brings the light of nature, the light of the moon and the stars which fades before the new morning light. Of this light St. Augustine says that it will never turn to darkness unless the Creator is abandoned by the love of his creatures. But this, too, belongs to the rhythm of day and night. As Hölderlin says in "Patmos";

> and shamefully
> A power wrests away the heart from us;
> For the Heavenly each demand sacrifice,
> But if it should be withheld,
> Never has that led to good.

301 When all visible lights are extinguished one finds, according to the words of the wise Yajñavalkya, the light of the self. "What then is the light of man? Self is his light. It is by the light of the self that a man rests, goes forth, does his work and returns." [12] Thus, with Augustine, the first day of creation begins with self-knowledge, *cognitio sui ipsius*,[13] by which is meant a knowledge not of the ego but of the self, that objective phenomenon of which the ego is the subject.[14] Then, following the order of the days of creation in Genesis, comes knowledge of the firmament, of the earth, the sea, the plants, the stars, the animals of the water and air, and finally, on the sixth day, knowledge of the land animals and of *ipsius hominis*, of man himself. The *cognitio matutina* is self-knowledge, but the *cognitio vespertina* is knowledge of man.[15] As Augustine describes it, the *cognitio*

---

[12] Brihadāranyaka Upanishad, IV, 3, 6 (cf. Hume, *The Thirteen Principal Upanishads*, p. 133).

[13] "And when it [the creature's knowledge] comes to the knowledge of itself, that is one day" (Et hoc cum facit in cognitione sui ipsius, dies unus est).—*The City of God*, XI, vii. This may be the source for the strange designation of the lapis as "filius unius diei." [Cf. *Mysterium Coniunctionis*, pp. 335, 504.]

[14] "Since no knowledge is better than that by which man knows himself, let us examine our thoughts, words, and deeds. For what does it avail us if we are to investigate carefully and understand rightly the nature of all things, yet do not understand ourselves?"—*Liber de Spiritu et Anima*, LI (Migne, *P.L.*, vol. 40, cols. 816–17). This book is a very much later treatise falsely attributed to Augustine.

[15] "Wherefore the knowledge of the creature, which is in itself evening knowledge, was in God morning knowledge; for the creature is more plainly seen in

matutina gradually grows old as it loses itself in the "ten thousand things" and finally comes to man, although one would expect this to have happened already with the onset of self-knowledge. But if this were true, Augustine's parable would have lost its meaning by contradicting itself. Such an obvious lapse cannot be ascribed to so gifted a man. His real meaning is that self-knowledge is the *scientia Creatoris*,[16] a morning light revealed after a night during which consciousness slumbered, wrapped in the darkness of the unconscious. But the knowledge arising with this first light finally and inevitably becomes the *scientia hominis,* the knowledge of man, who asks himself: "Who is it that knows and understands everything? Why, it is myself." That marks the coming of darkness,[17] out of which arises the seventh day, the day of rest: "But the rest of God signifies the rest of those who rest in God." [18] The Sabbath is therefore the day on which man returns to God and receives anew the light of the *cognitio matutina.* And this day has no evening.[19] From the symbological standpoint it may not be without significance that Augustine had in mind the pagan names of the days of the week. The growing darkness reaches its greatest intensity on the day of Venus (Friday), and changes into Lucifer on Sat-

---

God than it is seen in itself."—*Dialogus Quaestionum LXV*, Quaest. XXVI (Migne, *P.L.*, vol. 40, col. 741).

[16] The *Liber de Spiritu et Anima* attributes very great importance to self-knowledge, as being an essential condition for union with God. "There are some who seek God through outward things, forsaking that which is in them, and in them is God. Let us therefore return to ourselves, that we may ascend to ourselves. . . . At first we ascend to ourselves from these outward and inferior things. Secondly, we ascend to the high heart. . . . In the third ascent we ascend to God" (chs. LI–LII; Migne, *P.L.*, vol. 40, col. 817). The "high heart" (*cor altum;* also "deep heart") is the mandala divided into four, the *imago Dei,* or self. The *Liber de Spiritu et Anima* is in the mainstream of Augustinian tradition. Augustine himself says (*De vera religione LXXII*, Migne, *P.L.*, vol. 34, col. 154): "Go not outside, return into yourself; truth dwells in the inner man. And if you find that you are by nature changeable, transcend yourself. But remember that when you transcend yourself, you must transcend yourself as a reasoning soul."

[17] "Evening descends when the sun sets. Now the sun has set for man, that is to say, that light of justice which is the presence of God."—*Enarrationes in Ps. XXIX*, II, 16 (trans. Hobgin and Corrigan, I, p. 308). These words refer to Ps. 30 : 5 (A.V.): "Weeping may tarry for the night but joy cometh in the morning."

[18] *The City of God,* XI, viii. Cf. also *Dialog. Quaest. LXV*, Quaest. XXVI.

[19] *Confessions* (trans. Sheed), p. 289.

urn's day. Saturday heralds the light which appears in full strength on Sun-day. As I have shown, Mercurius is closely related not only to Venus but more especially to Saturn. As Mercurius he is *juvenis*, as Saturn *senex*.

302 It seems to me that Augustine apprehended a great truth, namely that every spiritual truth gradually turns into something material, becoming no more than a tool in the hand of man. In consequence, man can hardly avoid seeing himself as a knower, yes, even as a creator, with boundless possibilities at his command. The alchemist was basically this sort of person, but much less so than modern man. An alchemist could still pray: "Purge the horrible darknesses of our mind," but modern man is already so darkened that nothing beyond the light of his own intellect illuminates his world. "Occasus Christi, passio Christi." [20] That surely is why such strange things are happening to our much lauded civilization, more like a *Götterdämmerung* than any normal twilight.

303 Mercurius, that two-faced god, comes as the *lumen naturae*, the Servator and Salvator, only to those whose reason strives towards the highest light ever received by man, and who do not trust exclusively to the *cognitio vespertina*. For those who are unmindful of this light, the *lumen naturae* turns into a perilous *ignis fatuus,* and the psychopomp into a diabolical seducer. Lucifer, who could have brought light, becomes the father of lies whose voice in our time, supported by press and radio, revels in orgies of propaganda and leads untold millions to ruin.

[20] *Enarrationes in Ps. CIII,* Sermo III, 21 (Migne, *P.L.,* vol. 37, col. 1374).

THE COLLECTED WORKS OF
C. G. JUNG

EDITORS: SIR HERBERT READ, MICHAEL FORDHAM, AND GER-
HARD ADLER; *EXECUTIVE EDITOR*, WILLIAM McGUIRE. *TRANS-
LATED BY* R.F.C. HULL, EXCEPT WHERE NOTED.

IN THE FOLLOWING LIST, dates of original publication are given in pa-
rentheses (of original composition, in brackets). Multiple dates indicate
revisions.

(*continued*)

2. (*continued*)

(continued)

(*continued*)

(*continued*)

LIBRARY OF CONGRESS CATALOGING-IN-PUBLICATION DATA

Jung, C. G. (Carl Gustav), 1875-1951.

Aspects of the masculine/C. G. Jung; translated by R.F.C. Hull ;

introduction by John Beebe.—1st Princeton/Bollingen pbk. ed.

p. cm.

"From the Collected works of C. G. Jung, volumes 4, 5, 7, 8, 9 i,

10, 13, 14 (Bollingen series XX); C. G. Jung: letters (Bollingen

series XCV); C. G. Jung speaking (Bollingen series XCVII); C. G. Jung:

seminar on dream analysis (Bollingen series XCIX)"—Prelim. p. [i].

ISBN 0-691-01884-7

1. Masculinity (Psychology) I. Beebe, John. II. Jung, C. G.

(Carl Gustav), 1875-1961. Works. English. 1953.

Pantheon/Princeton. III. Bollingen series. IV. Title.

BF23.J763 1953

[BF692.5]

150.19′54 s—dc19

[155.3′32]   88-37903